What Your Boss Won't Tell You— Marilyn Moats Kennedy Will!

Have you just taken a new job—and is it the *wrong* job? Are you being passed up for promotion because of a "not-with-it" lifestyle? Do you lack vital technical skills, and can you read the subtle signals your superiors and co-workers are sending out?

Here, in a style both lively and informative, is *the* career guidebook for the eighties—one that lets you re-evaluate your own job attitudes and the problems of your organization with probing questions and self-tests, plus gives you the winning strategies you need to succeed...

CAREER KNOCKOUTS
How To Battle Back

Also by Marilyn Moats Kennedy

Office Politics: Seizing Power/Wielding Clout

Published by
WARNER BOOKS

CAREER KNOCKOUTS

How To Battle Back

Marilyn Moats Kennedy

WARNER BOOKS

A Warner Communications Company

WARNER BOOKS EDITION

Copyright © 1980 by Marilyn Moats Kennedy
All rights reserved.

This Warner Books Edition is published by arrangement with
New Century Publishers Inc., 275 Old New Brunswick Road,
Piscataway, N.J. 08854

Warner Books, Inc.,
75 Rockefeller Plaza,
New York, N.Y. 10019

 A Warner Communications Company

Printed in the United States of America

First Printing: February, 1982

10 9 8 7 6 5 4 3 2 1

DEDICATION

All for Daniel J.

Contents

Acknowledgments

When I began writing this book, hard on the heels of *Office Politics: Seizing Power/Wielding Clout*, the research seemed formidable. It was. Without the assistance of David Beasley, a senior at Northwestern University's Medill School of Journalism, the book would never have been finished by deadline. He spent a great many hours interviewing the willing and the reluctant, running down facts, and then rechecking them. He did a yeoman job.

Norma Green, who did most of the technical editing, also made a major contribution. She offered many valuable editorial suggestions, helped with structure and organization, and generally got the manuscript into readable form. Deborah Panter, who worked with me on *Office Politics*, came in for some last minute assistance as we moved toward deadline.

As usual, my husband, Daniel J. Kennedy, Jr., stoically suffered through major dislocations in our domestic life and vacation plans, not to mention providing all kinds of proofreading assistance and feedback. He did this with good cheer, encouragement, and willingness verging on sainthood.

My typing service, ESA, of Wilmette, Illinois—especially Nancy Johnson and Debbie Troester—continued cheerfully to grind out fresh chapters from illegible copy, seven days a week, under impossible deadlines.

Of course, Elaine Goldberg, managing editor of Follett Publishing Company, provided counsel and encouragement. I am extremely grateful to all of these people.

Most of the companies we interviewed for this book asked—indeed insisted on—not being acknowledged. This was especially true when they spoke off the record about such issues as reverse discrimination, age discrimination, and job obsolescence. One man we talked to asked us to destroy our notes once we'd put his material, suitably disguised, into the book. People from the Equal Employment Opportunity Commission really need not call us. We did as the gentleman asked. These firms deserve my thanks and I have thanked them privately, even if I cannot do so publicly.

It is my hope that the people who read this book will be encouraged about their individual career prospects in the 1980s. In a way the book is dedicated to American workers at all levels, as long as they have bosses. These workers should be encouraged. The 1980s aren't going to be anything like the 1960s but they are certainly going to be much better than the 1990s. But that's another book . . .

Even with a high inflation rate, a deepening energy crisis, organizational cutbacks and reorganizations, the career planner who works smart instead of just hard can move ahead. Keep in mind that even during the Great Depression there were people who made money—people who moved ahead of the crowd. These people simply didn't make the headlines as often as did those who were taking it on the chin.

Of course, all of the views expressed in this book are entirely my own. I take full responsibility for them. The examples were contributed either by the people we interviewed or by Career Strategies clients —a group of about 14,400 people I've worked with over the past five and a half years. I've changed all of the individual and corporate names to protect both the guilty and the innocent. I've even used material from some anonymous letters I've gotten following some of the many public career-planning seminars I've conducted. They usually begin, "I know you think you've heard it all, but let me tell you what happened to me . . ." Thank you all.

Marilyn Moats Kennedy
Evanston, Illinois

CAREER
KNOCKOUTS

Introduction: Looking for Land Mines

Career planning in the 1980s is going to change considerably from the focus it has had to date. It no longer is possible to limit planning to getting into the right organization and moving up because the people who turn to career planners for help have a growing number of needs. First, there is no one *right* organization, and, second, moving up is going to be much more difficult in the 1980s.

Getting a job is only the tip of the iceberg. The alternatives are not black and white, unemployment or nirvana, moving ahead or falling behind. There is a need to examine the ongoing process of rewinning and reshaping the job each working day. There is a need to look at ways of squeezing satisfaction from

1

work and that process hasn't been talked about much, if at all.

The fact is that most people under forty have a very different set of attitudes and expectations about work than do those over forty. There has been a significant change in work attitudes in just one generation. Few men in their sixties or seventies are going to understand the tremendous need of people under forty to like, even love, what they do for a living. To that older group it was enough to have steady work. If that work was really interesting, that was a bonus. Lack of interest was to be regretted but tolerated. Shaped as these older workers were by the Great Depression, liking and loving work never held a candle to job security and a regular paycheck.

The under-forty crowd wants a great deal more from work; they have both different and much higher expectations. Salary is only one issue and often not the most important one. The post-Viet Nam generation has an intense, emotional relationship to work that would certainly surprise the security- and paycheck-conscious older workers. When you read the chapters on "Emotional Satisfaction," "Job Hopping," and "The Killer Bs: Blockage, Boredom, and Burnout," you will see how different these relationships are. Many companies whose top management was shaped by the Depression are struggling to catch up with these changing attitudes and to understand them.

Not that top management makes a habit of trying

to understand new worker attitudes; this happens only when the impact of these attitudes hits the bottom line. Honesty is so far down the list of priorities for both workers and managers that it could be said to have disappeared entirely. Not honesty in terms of theft or chicanery, but honesty in terms of a mutual voicing of needs and concerns. For all the talk of human resource specialists, facilitators, and seminars in communication, both management and the worker seem determined to say what they think will sell, regardless of any hidden agenda or views. As much as any other single factor, this deception has an effect on the working lives of all of us.

The problems of organizations, both profit-making and non-profit-making, defy generalization, just as do the values of individual managers. However, in assessing the situation, certain patterns emerge. Although all organizations with be affected by the economic climate of the 1980s and the change in worker values, there seems to be no appreciable awareness of the tremendous impact that changing worker values will have on organizations. Many personnel professionals and top managers fail to see any differences between workers under forty and those over forty. Those who do see differences, seldom talk about them.

However, our concern is not with the organization but with the individual: his or her needs, problems, and the land mines that await. We are looking at crises, some preventable and some inevitable.

Traditional career planners and career-planning

literature address two issues: how to decide what you want to do (including goals, choosing organizations, and advancement potential) and how to get hired to do it. Having chosen a career and gotten hired, the worker is deposited at the organization's door, presumably safe until a change is needed or wanted, at which time career planners reappear. The question of what may happen to the worker who has actually begun working at the job is not addressed except in passing. It can't all be smooth sailing. There are so many land mines one can step on without warning. What are they? What kinds of career knockouts will the unsuspecting—or even the suspecting—worker meet in the short and the long run?

CAREER KNOCKOUTS

There are a number of identifiable crises—we've called them *career knockouts*—people meet that threaten job satisfaction or even destroy it entirely. These crises may threaten an individual's job tenure or even the ability to get another job should he or she fail at the first one. Most career knockouts are outside the realm of traditional career counseling and light-years ahead of what passes for vocational counseling in most high schools, colleges, and universities. Many of these institutions still think of career planning as vocational testing; they think of career planning as job hunting.

4

Many of the career crises we've identified require decisions with long-range consequences for people's career and job satisfaction. Many of these decisions are likely to be made under the pressure of the moment or even out of a sense of desperation by people who have only a fuzzy idea of the issues involved, if they have any idea at all. A great many don't. Where would they have gotten such knowledge? These decisions deserve some attention and thought during calmer times—before a job or career is on the line.

Some of the crises addressed in this book are hidden in the short run. You may have a career handicap of which you are totally unaware. Your career may not appear to suffer until some event or series of events spotlights a previously hidden, critical weakness. This may result in your being denied a promotion or refused employment.

All of these crises can be career knockouts. They can slow your progress in whatever direction you are going or they can result in termination. None is going to improve your performance, self-esteem, or morale. If you are fired, you may never be told the real reason in any words that make sense. That lack of a clear explanation is one of the genuine problems every worker faces. Hence, there is a need to look at your own working life and professional style with objectivity—to measure them against a standard apart from your own values. Your values are critical to you, of course, but they may keep you from seeing yourself as others see you; they may keep you from judging your work and work-style as others judge them.

The standards of judgment described in this book are composites based on research and interviews with thousands of people who make the decisions and shape the policies that affect other people's careers—primarily managers at all levels who develop policy and personnel people who, as enforcers, implement policy. We've interviewed only the people who have both the power to set standards and the power to enforce them. Without the power of potential enforcement, opinions on behavior and strategy are of academic interest only. As in *Animal Farm,* the novel by the British writer George Orwell, everyone may have opinions, but some opinions are more equal than others. You need to know about the "more equal" opinions.

SELF-EVALUATION AND EVALUATION OF OTHERS

The critical skills you must develop to protect and advance your career in the 1980s are the skills of self-evaluation and of assessment. Sometimes you'll think you need the help of divine revelation to understand the criteria on which other people base judgments of you the worker and you the human being. As you will learn, people afflicted with a particular career problem are often the last to know, if they ever manage to figure it out! Where is the person with the courage to tell a peer or subordinate that he or she is personally obsolete? Most people are completely, legitimately ignorant of such problems. No one tells them anything. The potential for anxiety and frustration in such situations is limitless. These sufferers may also color otherwise correct readings of the judgments of others by subjecting them to the ultimate career killer, the test of fairness and rightness.

You know the tune to this song because you and many of your coworkers sing it every time someone you don't respect gets promoted or a policy you despise is carved on the corporate tablets. The chorus goes, "It's not fair. It's not right. It shouldn't be that way."

If your boss honestly and consistently explained why what you were doing was going to slow down your career with the organization or even kill it entirely, you wouldn't need this book or the investigative and self-evaluative techniques it proposes. Unfortunately, honesty is seldom part of performance appraisal or even of informal conversation—especially as people touch delicate, personal, and even illegal, areas.

For example, what should you do if you are a thirty-year-old male and your boss tells you that you won't be promoted for four or five years because the organization is playing catch-up with its women and minority employees at your expense? You'd proba-

7

bly be screaming reverse discrimination to everybody at 110 decibels within a minute. How could it possibly benefit your boss, not to mention the organization, to level with you? If you didn't sue the organization, at the very least you'd change jobs. You probably wouldn't do this quietly, either. You'd be foolish to stick around. If the boss says nothing, counting on your misreading the signals, your dislike of job hunting (who doesn't dislike this chore?) and plain old inertia would probably keep you at the job, producing at your usual high level, blithely assuming that you were making progress. Your boss's duty is clear. Keeping you in the dark is good for the bottom line; it is good management on his or her part.

If you are a nice person, productive, easy to get along with, but lacking any semblance of working class, how can your boss tell you? It's not easy to tell someone that he or she is a closet case—not equipped socially to meet important customers or clients. You might argue, sue or leave. Any number of undesirable consequences come to mind. Why should your employer take such an unnecessary risk? If you are not told specifically what's holding you back, even if you have suspicions, there is nothing concrete on which you can focus. You may stick around simply because your pride has been saved. You are treated nicely, if paternally. Women are especially vulnerable to this sort of strategy. A little stroking can buy a lot of organizational peace.

ASSESSING THE FIELD

Half the battle in protecting your career is being able to identify the career knockout that may affect you rather than someone else in an almost unlimited and largely nameless field. It's often a process of elimination. This process is complicated by the fact that new candidates for career knockout of the month pop up while you're doing your research. Getting at the truth requires a high degree of investigative skill coupled with a high degree of skill in, and tolerance for, self-evaluation—not to mention a high tolerance for pain. You cannot depend on honest evaluations or reactions from anyone. You must be able to stand outside of yourself, bottle up your ego, and test your assumptions against other people's standards—however arbitrary and petty those standards seem. (It's time for another chorus of "It's not right, it's not fair . . .") No one expects you to embrace, adore, and live up to those standards if they are not right for you. There are always alternatives to consider. Understanding is always entirely separate from any action you might take, but understanding must precede any action you consider.

You and your boss will always be working at cross purposes. Your boss wants greater productivity at lower cost without hassles. He or she would be happier with thinking robots. You, despite your talk of your willingness to work harder, want greater opportunity for advancement without greater expenditure of effort. In this head-to-head conflict, the boss always holds the better cards. He or she has the power to enforce his or her personal and professional values on you as the price of your job or career advancement. Your alternatives consist of adapting to these values or changing them for a different set. This usually means turning in an old boss for a new one. If you don't understand which values are controlling in a particular situation, your career will suffer setbacks before you pick up the hidden signals.

No More Head in the Sand

The only way you can possibly control your career direction is to stand outside yourself and see a mirror image of what others see. If you can't do this, you will potentially face each career knockout described in this book. Thinking about it tomorrow may be less anxiety-producing, but the 1980s don't lend themselves to such a head-in-the-sand approach. If you are between twenty-five and forty, you are facing increasing competition from the baby boomers, already restless from what they see as too many people chasing too few good jobs. Affirmative action is an increasing force in management's decision-making process. The baby boomers are taking it on the chin and they are not happy about it.

It's going to require greater adaptability and dedication to get the kind of job that those now in their forties and fifties felt was no more than their due when they were in their twenties and thirties. Increased competition doesn't necessarily bring the cream to the top, grease also rises. Increased competition does, however, put tremendous strain on any organization's political system. Some sophistication in office politics is essential. You are going to work harder for proportionately fewer dollars. It doesn't take a crystal ball or clairvoyance to predict this. The signs have been around for at least ten years. If you are currently employed you may not realize this. After all, during the Great Depression any job was the goal. If you are not keeping up with inflation, you may be in your own personal depression right now. For example, a teacher who started working in 1970 for $8,400 and makes $12,600 in 1980 has had a 50 percent salary increase. That teacher, after his or her salary has been adjusted for inflation, is actually making 25 percent less, in terms of buying power, than he or she did in 1970. That's a personal depression and it's not limited to teachers. People in other nonprofit organizations have lost as much as 50 percent of their buying power through inadequate raises.

The Incredible Shrinking Dollar

It's possible that the annual inflation rate may reach 20 to 25 percent by 1985. If that happens, particularly if there are government wage and price controls, your raises will probably fall behind the inflation rate. You'll have to accept new realities. The only way to beat the system is to change job titles or jobs more frequently. You are going to face cutbacks, reorganizations, mergers, and closings as businesses and nonprofit organizations scramble to keep going. Without a much more sophisticated understanding of both economics and career management, your career can be undermined without your realizing what's happened.

The outlook is not totally bleak nor is the competition as great as it seems initially. Even among the baby boomers, a great many people aren't that ambitious to begin with. They go through the motions and pay lip service to advancement because it's expected. Some are getting greater social support for a less ambitious approach to work. There's even a trend for people in their twenties and thirties to take sabbaticals while they are young and unencumbered enough to experiment. They will then rejoin the work force and work until they are in their seventies and beyond.

However, if you do aspire to the top of whatever organization you've chosen to work for, you need to know where the career knockouts are. Keep in mind that organizations, like people, change constantly. You can adapt to these changes and do well no matter what the economic situation or the tenor of global politics. You will need a map to help you identify the land mines. That's what this book is all about.

Chapter 1
The Wrong Choice

Job hunting is always traumatic. The months of looking for just the right opportunity; the résumés; the letters written and rejections received; all the nerve-wracking interviews with people as bored as you are numb. Finally, a hit. You've found what appears to be a really good opportunity. The salary is close to what you had in mind or at least something reasonable. The people you'll be working with seem no more than ordinarily neurotic. Your boss seems to lean to the right side of competent. You begin.

On the first day some of your new coworkers take you to the first coffee break or invite you to lunch. The conversation is the usual sharing of unofficial but significant information, who's who and where to find things. You experiment a momentary chill. Suppose you've made the wrong choice? You repress the thought and concentrate on the conversation around you. The thought pops up again. You shudder, invisibly, you hope. The thought won't go away. Maybe this isn't the job you should have taken. Maybe you should have kept looking or chosen differently. But if that's the case, what do you do now?

Every job hunter can expect, at least once in a working lifetime, to make the wrong choice without realizing it until he or she is on site and beginning to work. There is probably nothing so shattering to the ego or so devastating to the morale as that realization. It's not just having made the wrong choice or even having used poor judgment that causes the panic, it's the sensation of being really and truly trapped. The common belief is that, even if you made a bad choice, you'll have to stay with the job for at least a year so that your next employer won't think you are a job hopper. Real masochists insist you stay two years—sort of a combination of punishment and expiation. That's nonsense and doesn't address the real issue at all.

NEW JOB BLUES

Did you make a bad choice or are you suffering from the new job blues? What options do you have if you have made a mistake? You are not trapped unless you've signed an employment contract and even then only if all the smart lawyers in your town are dead or on strike.

Most people have a period of depression as they begin a new job. This runs counter to the popular wisdom that says beginning a new job should be an emotional high. What people really experience is a combination of relief at finally having found a berth and a form of postpartum depression. It's the letdown that follows the end of the search. There's no longer a need for the artificial high and positive thinking you needed as you were hunting. There is often a sharp emotional bump as you adjust to a new workaday world. So far so good.

The problem arises when you are forced to confront the gut feeling that the choice you've made is not going to work out. You have no evidence to support this. No one has said or done anything to make you feel that the new job isn't going to be a good experience. It's usually an irresistible gut reaction.

CHANGE OF CAST

Some people may have a concrete reason for concern. Jackie arrived at her new job on the first day to find the unanticipated. The manager who'd hired her and with whom she'd seemed to have a workable rapport had given notice a week after Jackie had been hired. Since there had been a three-week lag between Jackie's being hired and the time she started the job, she arrived to find the department in a state of flux. No one was really in charge; no new manager had been named. There was fierce jockeying for position within the ranks.

It was obvious that the manager had been job hunting herself. Jackie felt both betrayed and irrationally angry at the organization. Jackie's plight is a common one. Most people try to do their jobs up to the very moment they announce their departures. Others, such as the manager who hired Jackie, elect to do the job until they report to the next job even if others see this as working under false pretenses This is how Jackie interpreted the manager's actions.

Jackie's problem is not ordinarily preventable. It would be difficult for an interviewer to tell a prospect that he or she was leaving. Any prudent job hunter would turn down an offer to work for an unknown person: it's always better to go for another interview after a successor has been chosen and the dust has settled.

Even if you take every precaution you can think of to make a sensible decision, there are times when you make mistakes or bad luck intervenes. Your gut feelings will not be denied; the sooner you face this the better. Until you face that fact, you are going to be paralyzed by anxiety, mourning, self-pity, and a whole range of emotions that dictate inaction and avoidance just when you need to gather all of your emotional strength for action. You will suffer more than you need to.

Like all myths, the one that dictates that you've got to stick to a new job once you've made a choice is hard to kill off. What will you tell your next prospective employer when asked why you left a job after only two weeks or three months? It's such an indecently short time. What will you tell your friends or spouse, or both? Thoughts of "wishy-washy," "indecisive," and even "immature" spring to mind unbidden. Despite this anxiety, the need to escape before your situation deteriorates and you are fired is greater than the need for a facile explanation.

"It Was Like This"

What appears to bother people most in this situation is not what is really happening but how to talk about it. The pressure to explain is enormous. At least ten of the job hunter's friends know of at least one poor soul to whom the very same thing happened. Naturally it was dreadful. That person was unemployed for months; developed wall-to-wall zits, tics, rashes, ulcers, and heartburn; was left by a spouse or lover; and ended up nearly wrecked. Our research indicates that almost every working adult has one aggressively neurotic friend who could behave this way. Since you are only ordinarily disturbed, why make comparisons? Hopefully you're more sensible, have rejected suffering as an art form or entertainment, and want to get on with straightening out your career.

Silence Is Golden

What do you tell your family and friends? Nothing. It's always the best and simplest explanation. Grit your teeth and keep quiet until you have something substantive to say. People will keep asking you why you are leaving a job after three weeks after you spent three months interviewing people in the organization and had been wildly enthusiastic only days before. Say, "I made a mistake in choosing the job. Now I'm in the process of correcting it." Speak firmly in a tone that implies that you have given all available information. Then ask your questioners for the names of some companies and/or people you should call. If you keep the conversation going, you will only entangle yourself in details and embroil yourself in a discussion that has moved from facts to emotions. Kennedy's Rule: *Honestly tell some how you feel and he or she will tell you why you shouldn't, couldn't, or don't really have the feelings you described*.

For example, if you say, "There's nobody in my department even remotely like me. They all have different educational backgrounds and have more experience. Maybe the manager made a mistake." Your friends will certainly respond with, "Well, that's their problem; you're in good shape," or, "You're imagining things."

Our research with job hunters indicates that more than 90 percent of the people who have made the wrong choice realize it within three weeks. That's about the length of time it takes to gain a minimal familiarity with the job and to get some feel for the work environment. Although this acclimation process may take as long as six months, depending on the job, it usually takes from three weeks to three months. Until you've been on site for about three weeks, all of your intellect is absorbed in just getting a feeling for the organization physically and politically.

Of that 90 percent, 46 percent are fired for cause within six to nine months. If you find you have made the wrong choice, that could be your fate. Take immediate steps to change your job, either within the organization or by moving to another organization.

People in this position are fired for not doing what they are being paid to do. Most of the people can't do the job for one reason or another, even though some of the reasons are entirely outside their control. Unfortunately, those who are fired will sustain real ego damage. Ego-damaged job hunters are always at a disadvantage when compared with reasonably confident applicants. Interviewers don't conduct group or individual therapy; they respond to externals only and can't have any clue as to your fragile emotional state or its causes.

Let's look at the issues in examining whether you've made the wrong choice. There are three major ones you'll need to look at carefully. First, did you really make the wrong choice? Second, if you did, where did you go wrong? Third, what can you do to rectify the situation right away?

ACCEPTING THE FACTS

Did you really make the wrong choice? If it feels that way, you probably did but let's look at your evidence more closely. Nobody wants to keep changing jobs just because they "feel" that things aren't right. You need a more substantial reason than that. As we said, postpartum depression is a very real part of the process of adjusting to a new job. It should lift within two to four weeks. If you are not getting some pleasure from your work or at least from the people environment at work, you probably have made the wrong choice. You might differ substantially in skills level, education, experience, or background from your peers who do the same job; that's a problem. The department or job may be totally different from what you expected. The department may be in the throes of a political war or a major reorganization.

So, you did indeed make a wrong choice. It may have been merely in the choice between taking that particular job and refusing it. It may have been a choice between two jobs. No matter, your feelings are not the result of the new job blues or of a momentary letdown. Somehow you must unravel your own decision to find out how that choice was made and why it is wrong.

You can learn something about yourself as a human being and a worker by examining the situation. If you shy away from this process you may end up repeating your error. This is not the time to blindly thrash around in a search for a quick and easy solution. So take the time to examine your decision.

WHAT WENT WRONG

Let's look at some of the most common causes for wrong choices. Of the 1,189 people in our sample, 30 percent caved in under external pressure or the expectations of others. This is a very common reaction. Regardless of a person's strength of character, it takes an almost superhuman effort to resist if enough people repeat something often enough. "But, you're great with people, such a good manager. Why would you want to do anything else?" The person who says, "I don't want to work with people. I'm burned out on all that," will invariably be contradicted. Most people profess to want to work with people; it's a job-hunting cliché. The unsure job hunter who seems to reject such a common value is cast in an unattractive light.

Add to this a few difficult interviews and a job you thought you really wanted that you didn't get. It's the ideal climate for a cave-in. People know they are caving in but hope that everything will work out once they begin the job. They are gambling against great odds.

Fully 25 percent of the people who reported a

mistake said that they had deluded themselves. As one man said, "I thought it was such a good job that I really should take it. Even though it wasn't in the area I'm best at or even very interested in, I agreed. I've never been so bored. Even the first week I knew I'd never make it in that job.

"What was really discouraging was that I didn't have anybody to blame but myself. I think part of my decision was based on how much my prospective boss seemed to want me."

People kidded themselves in two very common ways. They said either, "I can do anything I have to," or, "I can get along with anybody." People who kid themselves in these ways are setting themselves up for a fall more effectively than could any external nemesis. People who convince themselves intellectually of things that oppose gut responses will end up changing jobs more frequently. Generally they will also have a greater number of false starts.

Twenty percent of the people who made wrong choices underestimated the importance of salary. Money may not be everything (there is spirited argument on this point) but it is definitely a major determinant of lifestyle and the rise or decline thereof. People who tell themselves that they can live with a decrease in pay while they make a new start are rarely satisfied at the end of even the first month. Even those with a savings cushion, who are not actually suffering a spending decline, see themselves as somehow exploited. They see themselves as less than the people they were because they are being paid less.

It's hard to convince anyone, including yourself, that what you're paid on a job is not exactly what you are worth. It's progressively more difficult as time passes, and it's almost impossible to sustain after the sixth month. Job hunters agreed almost unanimously that none of them got used to less money. The only exceptions were a few people under twenty-five who had many unemployed or underemployed friends and several individuals making radical career changes, say from accounting to acting.

A factor as important as salary is job title. You thought you'd be called supervisor or manager; your boss calls you assistant supervisor or assistant manager. You were not given what you expected. Every time you say the word *assistant* your bonding to that job loosens a bit more. You didn't get the title in writing and therefore have nothing to prove it was promised. You'll be hating yourself, your boss, and the organization without letup in six months. This hardly increases your probability for success in the job.

"DID I MENTION . . ."

Fifteen percent of those who made the wrong choice got into a new job and confronted all of the preventables. These are the problems they'd forgotten to ask about during interviews or issues they hadn't raised. These people tended to go into interviews unprepared and wing it. For instance, they didn't ask what happened to predecessors, or how much after-work socializing was expected, or if employees had to eat in the company's windowless cafeteria. They ignored the potential for petty irritants to accumulate. They banked on their own flexibility and ability to roll with the punches.

The remaining 10 percent acted out of a real or perceived need to do something—anything—quickly. Once on the job, that desperation did not turn out to be a compelling enough reason to keep them from climbing the walls. This was especially true if their panic was financial or social. The panic tended to fade very quickly once the new job began; soon it was replaced by a new panic: the prospect of job failure.

AND NOW WHAT?

What do you do now? How can you gracefully extricate yourself from the job and move on with a minimum of damage to your career, your ego, and your other relationships?

The easy way out is to say, "Well, I made a mistake. I deserve this. I'll stick it out until I find something else or it finds me." That is unsatisfactory and simply puts off the problem. The job isn't going to work out. If you don't change jobs now, you may fail on the job and be fired outright or be forced to leave. Waiting means reducing your options. You're in the best position right now to get back to job hunting. Your job-hunting skills are still sharply honed. Your contacts are still fresh. Many people haven't heard that you've taken a job; they assume you are still looking. If you've turned down any jobs that look good in light of the one you did take, they may still be open. You may not want any of them, but if an organization thought enough of you to make an offer perhaps you could reestablish communication with your contacts there. Other openings may have come up since your last contact.

Step by step, here's how to extricate yourself from the job and move on with some semblance of grace.

Step One

Why was taking the job a mistake? There is no point in making the same or a similar mistake time after time; twice is at least once too often. You can't job hunt effectively until you know what went wrong. No inchoate longings, please. You have to be specific. There is a reason and you've got to identify it. If you can't put your finger (or pencil)) on the one reason, get a sheet of paper and start listing the original criteria you used to select the job. You should always have a written checklist of the political, environmental, and people factors you need to be happy and productive. This is your agenda when you interview a prospective employer. Many job hunters make the error of trying to keep this agenda mentally. That's always a mistake. Make a written list. You're under too much pressure in an interview to rely on your memory. Not that you'd pull out your checklist and pencil during an interview, but the minute you're released you must hotfoot it to a spot of safety and go over that list. As in most human affairs, prevention is everything, extrication always sticky.

Suppose you can't come up with a specific reason or reasons for your decision. Perhaps you can arrive at the answer through the back door. Put down on paper what was right about the job and compare your agenda with the list of good points. What's missing? If nothing strikes you, it's time for a more detailed breakdown. There are three parts to the job-disaster equation: 1) the tasks you are to do compared with your skills; 2) the people environment in which you must work, both your boss and your peers (this includes the "how" of the job, issues of style, and the political/social environment); and 3) the physical environment.

Put each heading—Tasks, Political/Social, and Physical—on a separate sheet of paper. Now list under each heading the pros and cons of the job. One woman could not explain her acute dissatisfaction until she got to the issue of physical environment. Despite her best efforts at self-discipline, she could not reconcile herself to working in an office with a bull-pen arrangement. She had wanted, and felt she needed, a private office. The open office with its utter lack of privacy and desks cheek by jowl left her irritable, unproductive, and distracted.

Nothing in the job could make up for the lack of privacy and visual peace. She put physical environment at the top of her list for a renewed search.

Once you establish the root cause or causes of your dissatisfaction, it's time to move to step two.

Step Two

Should you quit this job and look full-time again? The temptation is often to pretend that you never took the job in the first place. After all, you've only been there three weeks, or three months, so why not wipe the slate clean and pretend that you've been job hunting all along?

This course of action has one serious flaw and a lot of "flawlets." The serious flaw is that it is not true. Naturally, you're not going to invite people to ask questions by putting a job you worked at for only three weeks at the top of your résumé. However, denying that you ever took the job is a lie. It can be disguised on the résumé but it cannot be left off the application unless you're prepared to risk being fired from your next job. If your deception is discovered, as it almost inevitably will be, you are likely to be fired. You might be interested in knowing that such a lie is rarely discovered through reference checks or other official channels. It's much more likely that you'll be found out through the informal network. Your boss will meet someone who worked with you at the short-term job or who knows that you had the short-term job.

Dave left his job in the tax department of a large

bank after six harrowing months during which he'd had three bosses and lived through an inept but very bloody reorganization. He decided to forget the job and not mention it to his prospects. Unfortunately, he'd been on his new job as a tax supervisor for only three months when one of his three former bosses was hired as a supervisor. The former boss, now a peer, not knowing that Dave had neglected to mention their mutual former employer, spilled the news within three hours of his arrival. The new boss was not pleased. Personnel got into the act and Dave was asked to resign.

The "flawlets" include having continually to remember your official line, the need to worry about references, and the internal pressure created by the risks.

If you're not going to lie what are you going to say? If asked why you quit the job after only three weeks or three months, you will say, "I realized early on that I had made a mistake in choosing that job. The only honorable thing to do was to correct it." You may as well put the mantle of honorable behavior around your shoulders. There's no point in feigning regret. You'll evoke fewer questions from an interview if you answer the question squarely without the tiresome explanations and disclaimers to which the interviewer is accustomed.

If the interviewer is after a more complex explanation, try to find out what's on his or her agenda. Most interviews, like most lovers, don't care to hear the details of past relationships. Only if an interviewer has been burned by someone with a similar work profile will he or she want to be assured that whatever was wrong with that person is not wrong with you. For instance if the last person the interviewer hired who'd left a job after three weeks turned out to be a chronic job hopper, you'll have to sell yourself and your job stability roughly twice as hard as would ordinarily be necessary. You may not make the sale. It will depend on how much aggravation your job twin caused.

Knowing that the stability question is bound to come up, you should couch all answers to questions that skirt the issues in terms reflecting your stability. You may want to violate a traditional job hunter's taboo and talk about your personal as opposed to professional stability if you can offer convincing evidence that you are usually very prudent in making decisions. Don't underestimate the interviewer's concern. The younger you are, the more concern the interviewer will have.

As you can see, how you talk about the job you've left is much more important than whether you quit or stayed until you got another job. Being unemployed for a few months or even a year has no long-term impact on your prospects *unless* it is indicative of another problem. In making the decision to leave immediately or to stay and try to job hunt, there are three very important considerations.

1. Can you make it financially if you are unemployed for from one week to six months? You cannot quit a job on the gamble that you'll have another in

a specific period of time. You simply can't cut it that close financially. Will you be able to get back on the unemployment compensation rolls immediately or will there be a lag? Are there any holidays (such as Christmas and New Year) or a heavy vacation time that might slow down your job hunting; perhaps people you need to interview with will be out of town?

Don't count on anything. You should have roughly twice as much money as your best estimate of what you'll need before you quit. Don't ever quit until you have secured health insurance; at today's prices, an uninsured ingrown toenail could bankrupt you. The exception: the job is making you so anxious or provides so much pressure that your health is in danger. You don't need a doctor or therapist to tell you this. If you are physically sick or mentally distressed, you've got to quit. Nothing is worth a physical or mental breakdown. You can always work the nightshift in a factory or work as a temporary during the day.

2. What are the difficulties you'll face in job hunting while trying to do the new job? Ordinarily, it's not too difficult to do your current job while surreptitiously job hunting. However, if you are shaky on the new job because the whole routine is unfamiliar, you may not be able to keep both balls in the air. Avoid being fired. You may be anyway but there's no reason either to invite or to hurry the process.

3. What are the stresses of the new job? If your dissatisfaction with it is so great that you really can't concentrate enough to present a confident, pulled-together exterior for interviewing, quit and look for a new job.

Only you can make these judgments. Don't be guided by the advice of people who can't get inside your skin and feel the way you feel, i.e., the advice of people who see only your confident facade. Don't kid yourself. Pressure may not kill job hunters but who'll say it does them any good?

If you decide to quit, give two weeks' notice. Always preserve good form. This leaves a good taste in the organization's mouth and keeps people from focusing on your untimely departure any more than is absolutely unavoidable. Thank everybody and try to give them as little feeling that they let you down as you can. This is no time to vent your angry feelings even if you have cause. Keep your explanation short and to the point. The job will not work out. It is not right for you. You need to spend all your time job hunting. Do not go into detail in the exit interview unless it would be a service to the company. Criticizing your boss or coworkers is rarely a service. If you were promised something that didn't materialize, you might mention that because that is something the personnel department might be able to do something about. You might mention working conditions if they were a problem. Other than that, keep quiet or it will go on the record that you were a malcontent. That you do not need.

Step Three

Begin your renewed search immediately. This time you are going to have to be more selective. Nobody's ego can stand two errors in a row. Get on the telephone to all of your contacts. Activate your network and let people know you're looking; don't say *looking again*. Keep the explanations as short as possible. The "I made a mistake and now I'm correcting it" routine is best. If someone pins you down, give them another sentence. Never discuss details or personal gripes. You can hold a postmortem after you've secured the next job. Doing so now would just confuse your contact people.

Go to as many trade and professional association meetings as you can and circulate. As long as the group's focus is even remotely related to what you want to do, there will be contacts who will know of openings. Spread yourself as thin as possible in terms of generating leads. Meet as many different people as you can. Don't spend a lot of time with clumps of people from the same organization. Follow up every single lead. The minute you know you're not interested, drop it. You have no time to waste. So many jobs are known about internally but are not advertised. There is no better source of information about this submerged market than the people who work for the organizations with the jobs.

You will find that these associations are listed in the Yellow Pages of the telephone directory in most cities. If the associations you need aren't in the phone book, call people engaged in the kind of work you're looking for in large companies and ask them when the particular trade association meets. Personnel departments in some large organizations can supply this information. If you don't know the names of the associations you need, go to the public library and look them up in the *Encyclopedia of Associations* or a similar reference book; you'll find such comprehensive guides a real help. You also may uncover some associations you didn't know existed.

According to our research, one out of ten leads turns up a real job opening. If you wanted to find ten live job openings, you'd need one hundred leads. Other than the trade and professional associations, there is no quick, inexpensive way to turn up one hundred leads. That's why they are so important. Job hunting quickly means accelerating the rate at which you find and discard possibilities. If you had unlimited time, you could rely on want ads or wait for your friends and colleagues who know you are job hunting to call. Since you're in a hurry, you need to do everything you can to generate leads on your timetable.

If you kidded yourself about salary the last time, don't put yourself in the path of temptation again. Before you schedule an interview, ask about the salary range. There is no point in getting excited about a job only to find out that the salary is $5,000 a year less than you could possibly accept. All that does is cause you to waste time, energy, and adrenalin on unproductive interviews.

If you find a job that you really want at a salary you can't live with, you have one of two options: get a commitment for an early salary review and get it in writing or decide you'll moonlight. Do not tell yourself you will "manage." That's what happened the first time and you didn't and couldn't. Lest this seem like an indictment of your self-discipline, keep in mind that the inflation rate, actual and forecast, is about 18 percent a year. There is no evidence—not even astrological—to suggest that this rate will drop much in the 1980s; smart money says it will increase to 20 to 25 percent by 1985. Even if you have extraordinary willpower, having eighteen cents or more removed from every dollar periodically will make a substantial difference in your ability to pay your bills.

Chapter 2
Working Class

In a classless society, dedicated to the proposition that "all men (and occasionally some women) are created equal," it's amazing how many people have very deeply held convictions about class—who has it and who doesn't. If these convictions remained carefully on the social, nonwork side of life, we'd refer you to Lelitia Baldridge's revised and expanded *The Amy Vanderbilt Complete Book of Etiquette*. Unfortunately, class is not interchangeable with etiquette. It is not a function of money, power, education, or even background. Lack of class can be a career knockout because it's the last frontier of the things "even your best friend won't tell you." And if your friends won't (or don't have enough themselves to know what you lack), you're not likely to get many clues about your problem from any but the most perceptive employer.

In surveying about seven hundred working adults, mostly middle managers and professionals, we found that etiquette, while important, was only the tip of the iceberg. Surprisingly, when asked for a definition of what constituted class, i.e., the criteria for distinguishing someone who had class from someone who didn't in a business situation, the results were startlingly similar.

WHO HAS CLASS?

Working class means a total style, one that appears both comfortable to you and comfortable for a majority of the people with whom you deal, people whose viewpoints range from extremely conservative to extermely liberal. Working class includes manners, attitudes, dress, consideration shown others, and personality.

A person who has class makes most of the people he or she deals with feel reasonably comfortable most of the time. The person consistently behaves in ways that are appropriate and considerate. Everybody has bad days but a person who has class has fewer or appears to have fewer. A person who lacks working class is either ignorant of, or indifferent to, the subtle reactions of others. He or she will work right through the long run completely unaware that he or she is not even remotely being considered for any higher position, having been written off years ago as not having "it."

In defense of the people who make the decisions, how would you like to tell someone that his or her style is at odds with the organization's style and values? It's equivalent to telling a blind person it's too bad he or she is blind. Most people don't realize that class behavior is learned and can be changed. It sounds so petty, so vague, so mean, and it's so terribly, critically real. The attitudes expressed in our survey toward behavior and appearance did not differ markedly when voiced by older, more conservative people or younger, less conservative ones. In fact, on three issues, all of our respondents were in accord.

THE LOOK OF SUCCESS

The way you dress in relation to whatever your business situation is the first way in which people judge your relative class standing. It is not a question of whether you are lower, middle, or upper class. It is a question of whether you do or don't have it. None of our respondents named the economic class to which anyone belonged. That seemed to be irrelevant. Comments ranged from, "When he came into my office wearing that pale lavender shirt with a tie which gravy would have improved, and a plaid suit so loud it could have doubled for a horse blanket, I knew he had no class. How could we send someone like that out to call on our bank customers? He's still with us but we consider him strictly an inside man," to "She always looks as if she had dropped into the office on the way to an orgy."

It wasn't the cost of the clothing people wore as much as the relative appropriateness of overall appearance to the role the person was expected to play. In fact, the attitude that clothing is packaging, not self-expression, seems to be gaining widely, even in relatively backwater areas. If John Molloy did nothing else in his *Dress for Success* books, he seems to have convinced a great many people that first impressions are vital and that through the choice of clothing individuals have more control over first impressions than they thought.

A great many women seem not to have picked up on John Molloy's message. Rather than seeking clothing that projects a businesslike attitude and that impresses others favorably, they still seem to be slavishly following *Vogue*. How else could one explain seven-inch heels on what are supposd to be shoes-to-wear-to-work? Or skirts slit within an inch of the vice squad? Many women deem inappropriate clothing as worth fighting for—career be damned!

Homemade clothes that look it are dreadful. Unless your tailoring skills match those of Beene, Blass, or Klein, save your creative efforts for your private life. If you're spending a great deal of time making your business wardrobe, someone is bound to wonder why you're not putting that time into your work. Homemade ties and hand-sewn vests are out. If anyone asks if you made something you're wearing, don't wear it to the office again. In fact, all gimmicky, cutesy clothing, no matter what the source, should be left at home. Dress for the position you hope to occupy, not the one you have.

By the way, your teeth are "clothing" in a sense. If yours are decayed, crooked, stained, etc., they are unattractive, really unpresentable. You can't be too poor to afford dental care. Go to a university dental clinic or find a company with dental insurance. This isn't just a business handicap; your health is at stake.

Heavy on the Chocolate, Please

Being greatly overweight can make you unpromotable even though people don't say so. If you are from fifty to one hundred pounds or more over the norm you have a serious problem. The number of rotund corporate presidents and top-level executives of either sex we turned up was zero. Being overweight means that you are less presentable, less healthy, altogether less equipped to compete. Despite all of the popular magazine articles, people in our surveys tended to see overweight as a character weakness, not an illness. Right or wrong, the general impression is that fat people lack class. There is no lobby or law that protects the fat people of America from discrimination.

DESE, DEMS, AND DOSE

The second determinant was use of the spoken language. Two points came out during the survey. First, even people who cannot name the parts of speech in standard English can identify a grammatical error. Even people who made particular errors from time to time were able to pick out the error when it was made by others. It's the same thing as spelling in written prose; you can tell if a word is misspelled even if you can't spell it correctly. There is no explaining this double standard, but there's no point in pretending it doesn't exist either.

Furthermore, a person was consistently seen as more important, more powerful, and as having more class if he or she sounded like Walter Cronkite or Jane Pauley and less like the late Mayor Richard J. Daley of Chicago. Daley's speech patterns were not an affectation; they came naturally. Yet even in Daley's heyday it was not of particular advantage to ape Daley's speech. The many people who sound as he did often find it a real business disadvantage.

Any kind of extreme accent, one which deviates from the Cronkite/Pauley mold, is a liability even if nobody tells you so. If you sound like Daley or like Judy Holliday in the movie *Born Yesterday*, or even like the Fonz on "Happy Days," you have a problem. You are not, strictly, speaking, as presentable as people closer to the norm. People won't tell you this because they think you can't help it. You fall into the category of "more to be pitied than scorned."

Slang and swear words also create the wrong image. Too much slang and too many "expletives deleted" can put people off. There's still a double standard in regard to swear words; women use them less successfully, especially when in the company of older men. Why risk offending someone? If you never use swear words, you're less likely to offend.

Like, It's Real Heavy, Man

Such phrases as "you know?," "Okay?," and "like, you know" are the mark of an oral illiterate. Listen to yourself sometime; you may be appalled.

It is a fact that people who have inherited wealth, such as the Rockefellers, Morgans, Vanderbilts, etc., seldom sound as Mayor Daley did or as a self-made cattle baron from Oklahoma might. Preparatory schools are great levelers of language differences. Even the Boston accent of the Kennedys or the accents heard most often in certain boroughs of New York City don't travel cross-country very well. Outside the deep South, southern accents, especially those from Georgia, Louisiana, and Mississippi, bring to mind rednecks and good old boys, not business. President Carter's accent had not been an asset; it had been off-putting to the majority of the people with whom he associated.

What most people fail to recognize, though it is absolutely true, is that what Henry Higgins did for

Eliza Doolittle in *Pygmalion* was no miracle. Higgins's skill has been refined and passed on to speech therapists. Some of the methods described in the play are still used today. Nobody has to speak with an objectionable accent.

Changing one's speech patterns is not easy. It won't be cheap. It will require patience and a great deal of hard work. Still, if your career requires extensive public contact with people whose speech patterns differ greatly from your own, you should be aware of this option. You can always revert to your native speech patterns when appropriate.

The finest Saville Row tailoring, the finest grooming, even the right degree from the right school will not overcome a handicap that is apparent as soon as you open your mouth. Speech will undo your other assets because, as a nation, we still admire the Cronkite-Pauley model as standard American English.

Speech therapy can also help you if you stutter, screech, breathe improperly, speak in a monotone, or have any of a number of other handicaps. It's a mistake to think you can change speech patterns on your own. Many bad habits may respond to do-it-yourself cures; speech problems are not among them. Despite what people tell you, you can't overcome your handicaps with tapes and records in your spare time.

What you can do is learn better grammar and sentence structure. Just because your education neglected the parts of speech and sentence construction doesn't mean you can't learn them. Good grammar is a foundation upon which to build.

MANNERS

The third determinant was table manners. Poor or offensive table manners were seen as very detrimental. This is surprising when you think that only about one eighth or one ninth of the business day is engaged in eating or drinking; it is not surprising when you consider the number of deals put together over lunch, the clients wined and dined, and the cocktail parties given.

Table manners used to be handled by families who knew, or thought they knew, what was acceptable. During the twenties and thirties, when the hoi polloi infiltrated colleges, fraternities and sororities gave some of the less polished pledges a lesson or two. Unfortunately, in the sixties and early seventies, total lack of training—even informal training—became the norm.

Since young people were more concerned about the Viet Nam War and then about getting jobs, the whole issue of table manners went by the boards. The result is that a great many people between the ages of twenty-five and thirty-five had little training in table manners, good or bad. They're winging it. Many seem absolutely incapable of distinguishing between different forks, much less of understanding how to disjoint a chicken or handle spaghetti properly. They ignore napkins, speak with their mouths full, and start eating before others have been served. Imagine the effect on the sixty-year-old president of a company!

Since friends don't ordinarily point out any but the most blatant violations and business colleagues point out nothing, most people aren't even aware that they have a problem. Those who are aware don't quite know how to cope and so avoid situations they think will be difficult. One young man reported that he would rather starve than try to eat chicken or spaghetti publicly. That's a shame since they seem to be favorites for the business lunch. Half a chicken, fried or broiled, is the staple of the trade association and organization menu. If you don't know what to do, you may be hungry or embarrassed much of the time.

MR. X, MEET MR. Y

Following these three major determinants, survey participants listed other elements of class, which, while less important overall, could become very important in certain situations. The problem of introductions was mentioned frequently. Many people remember from childhood that introductions are usually made by introducing the more important person to the less important; older people to younger people; females to males. The problem is that many people don't think to introduce people to each other at all. It's fatal in a business situation because it marks you as socially illiterate. Always err on the side of too many introductions rather than too few. People can stop you if they've been introduced before. Shake hands with everybody, male and female. A man who doesn't offer his hand to a woman or vice versa is risking offense.

ONE FOR THE ROAD

Social drinking was another problem. A great many otherwise savvy people think they have to drink at cocktail parties or quasi-social occasions. This is not true. It's enough to give the appearance of drinking. This is especially the case when you might drink too much or appear tipsy simply because you haven't had enough to eat, are tired, are under stress, etc. The people who can't handle liquor gracefully seldom seem to realize it. If there is any doubt in your mind, skip the alcohol. As long as you're carrying a glass, nobody will question what's in it. If you have an alcohol problem, or think you do, get help today. Alcoholism is the ultimate career killer.

YOUR SCOTCH OR MINE?

Working class covers everything you do with the people you work with and for and that includes entertaining. There is no excuse for giving a Bring-Your-Own-Bottle party for peers or superiors, much less subordinates. People will probably come the first time. If *they* have any class, they won't remark on your cheapness, but they won't forget it. It's no party if guests have to pay. If you can't afford to entertain and pick up the tab, skip it.

If you're entertaining business associates, use a restaurant so that you can arrange all of the details in advance. Don't entertain at home unless you have or can get reliable help or are truly a host or hostess of distinction. By doing so you'd just be opening yourself up to all kinds of covert criticism that can't be useful to your career. The horror stories people have related when they've gone to other people's houses for dinner would fill an entire book.

If you do entertain at home, farm out your children and pets. An evening of watching your baby upchuck and your two-year-old scream or of being pawed by a hungry Saint Bernard can keep the grapevine in negative stories for weeks. Suffice it to say, if you don't know how to entertain or suspect that you don't, practice by entertaining your college chums, who are there to see you, not to judge your talents.

Keep in mind that entertaining people you work with and for is not a social occasion; it's strictly business. Don't be misled because people don't seem to talk exclusively about business. They'd all be somewhere else relaxing with pals if the necessity of business hadn't plopped them on your doorstep.

Learn enough about wine so that you can distinguish between brands and can order a decent wine if called on to do so. Take a course if necessary. At least rely on the wine steward to make a selection within a certain price range. The people who dismiss this as snobbery are usually the ones who end up entertaining snobs, maybe their bosses or clients.

BRING YOUR OWN ORANGE CRATE

Don't entertain anyone who's important to your career in your apartment if it's decorated in vintage Good Will and early Salvation Army. It brings to mind the question of whether or not you are the right person for the job or promotion. Maybe all you really want is the simple life. If they're paying you a good salary, the question as to what you're spending money on always comes up.

All the old rules are being rescinded. A bachelor who lives in squalor, can't cook or keep his wardrobe in order, is more to be scorned than pitied. Nobody thinks such behavior acceptable today. Maybe Julia Child doesn't invite herself to dine at your house on a regular basis; still, you had better be able to cook one or two company dinners if you're likely to be forced to have business guests at home. Broken crockery, chipped cups, and mismatched dime store stainless are not helpful reflections on your table.

Anytime someone who associates with you in business comes into your home, it's a business occasion. You are working just as much as if you were in the office. There is no distinction. That's why all of the rhetoric about "relaxing" and "being yourself" are worthless. Most business people fervently hope that no one is going to "be him- or herself." The prospect is terrifying. Decorum is better.

STRIKE THREE

Middle managers in banks and brokerage houses don't bowl and play softball, at least not on the company team. If you want to do those things, gather your old college pals, play with them, and don't talk about your scores. For business occasions, learn to talk knowledgeably about sports important to your peers—racquetball, tennis, handball. Better yet, learn to play.

SOME OF MY BEST FRIENDS

There has been a major change in attitudes toward expressed sex and race discrimination since the 1960s. It's not that people have changed their real feelings. A vast majority of men still secretly wish that women would bake bread and tend children at home than muck around in business. Some of these Neanderthals even have working wives. A great many white people probably still wish black people would stay in their own neighborhoods. They support the NAACP. The difference is that it's absolutely, unforgivably crass to say such things publicly. You'll never know that people are offended because they won't correct you or argue the point in a business situation. They'll simply mark you off as someone without class.

YES AND NO, MAYBE

There is an enormous difference between the technically correct answer and the appropriate answer. People who ask for your opinion (as opposed to a request for facts) want the appropriate answer, not the correct one. Forget candor; it's a career killer. Most of the people you work with and for want mercy, not justice. If you insist on meting out justice, you're hurting your own career, not someone else's. If you're asked how you'd feel about organizing a retirement party for the organization's least competent employee, the correct answer is that you wouldn't be interested, the appropriate answer is to ask when such a party is wanted and who is to be invited.

The difference between a business situation and a social situation is that people can choose not to see you socially. Your business associates can't always do that. Therefore, if you make them uncomfortable with your attitudes and behavior, they do one of two things: hold back promotions if they're powerful enough or talk about you unfavorably so that it reaches people who are powerful enough to hurt your career.

EXCEPT ROGER, OF COURSE

Everybody knows somebody who's successful in defiance of even the most basic rules of etiquette. Someone who loses his or her temper, makes people uncomfortable, or otherwise is a pain to deal with but is still powerful. That person probably got to his or her current position in the past, not in the 1980s. You don't have to be Isaiah to predict that problems with the economy and the ever-growing energy crisis are producing a much more conservative, sober business climate. Transplant the free thinker to the 1980s and he or she is liable to sink without a trace.

The fact that never seems to impress itself on most people who lack class is that nobody ever tells you that you have problems that are holding you back. It's probably the last frontier of reticence. You can ignore the whole problem, never test your own business and social skills, and wing it. However, in a bad economy, more class, not less, will be expected of the people who are retained and promoted. Rough edges paraded before bosses and peers are going to make for rough going in this decade; success calls for class.

NEUTRAL TOWARD ALL

The worst set of problems many people have are those that surround the forming of comfortable working relationships with people in the office. You do not have a right to like or dislike the people with whom you work. If there is one thing that people universally judge as tacky, it's withholding respect, consideration, and cooperation from people you dislike for whatever reason. Not only are you not a team player but you're exhibiting an unbelievable degree of pettiness. Don't do it. Save all of your strongest feelings and give them a workout after work, away from anyone connected with the office. Of course you're entitled to your opinions—the concern is where you express them.

Don't talk about your lifestyle, whatever it is. You may be half of a lesbian couple or the father of two toddlers. To the people who listen to you expounding, both styles are equally boring. Small talk should be as value free and as nonpersonal as you can make it. Protect your private life and develop and maintain some separation between your work and nonwork lives. You'll never make any converts to the true faith anyway.

Don't talk about your poverty level. Money is still a powerful taboo. People who constantly talk about how strapped they are financially make others extremely uncomfortable. People will cross the street to avoid you if you're known for your nonstop litany of poor-mouthing. If you're really in dire financial straits, get a better job or moonlight.

Keep your strongest opinions to yourself. Nobody cares, even the people who ask for them. It may seem cynical but it's true. Besides, why risk offending people who can harm you? Save them for people with whom you're really involved.

PICASSO WHO?

Don't fake an opinion. If you haven't read the book, seen the movie or play, or heard the music, don't think you can pretend because you read a review. It won't work unless you're talking to someone who is doing the same thing. Whoever asked if you had heard, read, or seen something is dying to tell you what he or she thought anyway. It's both prudent and tactful to let him or her do so.

If you don't know anything about literature, art, and music and you hope to rise above the ranks of middle management, learn. As society becomes more conservative, this kind of knowledge will again be an indicator of class. If all you can talk about is spectator sports, you are going to be the company bore at cocktail parties.

If you want to do your own thing exclusively, start your own business and sell to others who agree with you in every respect, providing always that you can find such people. Failing that, you are going to have to submerge your individuality to the extent that you blend in with the image people have of someone with working class. There will always be industries and individual organizations more tolerant of a diamond in the rough. If that's your style, you should be searching for one of them.

People who are late for appointments, unless rushed to the hospital by paramedics, are crass. Even if you have the power to make people wait, it's not a good use of that power to do so. Your subordinates not only judge you harshly and pass on their judgments, it also shows a lack of consideration and respect for those you are inconveniencing. This meanness on your part will make it all the way through the grapevine and back in a flash.

Smoking when nonsmokers are present is rude. It's not your privilege unless you don't care what others present think. In the 1980s, smoking should be an activity engaged in only in the privacy of your own home or strictly with consenting and participating adults.

Being publicly out of step with social values is a career killer because it calls attention to you in the least favorable way. Driving a gas guzzler during the energy crisis or having a fire in the fireplace in July and then running the air conditioning at its lowest setting to make the room comfortable are examples.

Finally, the Golden Rule has not been improved on as a guide to business behavior. "Do your own thing" and "let it all hang out" aren't quite in the same league.

Suppose you suspect that you are guilty of some, many, or, heaven forbid, most of the behaviors and attitudes about which we've been talking. What do you do? Where do you get assistance? Obviously, it would only compound the problem to ask any of your associates or business acquaintances for a performance appraisal in such delicate and taboo areas. However, in order to change, you will need some help and feedback. Don't ask your family and best friends. They like the real you. Get help only from someone you won't meet either professionally or socially. Check with community colleges; they offer courses in virtually everything. If you're supersensitive and don't want to enroll in a public course, track down some of these college instructors and ask if they will tutor you. Ditto with speech therapists.

Look at the people with whom you work. Is there anybody who could be a role model? Some offices are knee-deep in tacky people who vie with each other for honors in advanced crass. If that's your situation, look elsewhere. Who, among your friends, looks and behaves in ways that you identify as appropriate? Stalk this person (quietly) and try to analyze what he or she is doing.

Get an etiquette book and read it. Skip the parts that don't apply or that cover once-in-a-lifetime events. As you read, you'll see that there's an internal logic and point of view to the whole business. If it's just dawning on you that some of the things you do make others uncomfortbale, you'll have to experiment to find ways to change. Its going to take time.

You may want to hire someone to work with you on your clothing, your home, your speech, even your manners. (Yes, there are people who try to slick up the ordinary person.) It will be the best investment you ever made in yourself. People will notice. If this is too much self-improvement to tackle at once, pick out your greatest need and start there. If you have to make a choice, work on your speaking voice first. Then work on clothing. Next, tackle your manners, and finally your home. This is what people ought to mean when they say someone is "self-made."

Chapter 3
Lack of Emotional Satisfaction

"My work just doesn't give me the high it used to," David said. "I used to be thrilled to get up and go to work—wondering what excitement I'd generate that day. Now, it's just routine."

Marianne said, "Work is the most important part of my life. When someone says, 'Who are you?,' I say I'm a systems analyst. My work is me."

If there is one problem that will increasingly be characteristic of the twenty-five to thirty-five-year-old worker in the 1980s it will be the endless, frantic reaching for total emotional involvement with and satisfaction from work. It isn't productivity or work satisfaction that many people want from their jobs, it's a physical and emotional high. It's almost as if ordinary work satisfaction had lost out to a new way of thinking and feeling about what one does for a living. Such feelings have left many employers baffled as they see workers scrambling for more and greater highs.

WHERE DO YOU FIT?

Three kinds of satisfaction are to be derived from work. The first is internal; the feeling is self-congratulatory. "I did that very well, with skill," you say to yourself or, "God, I'm good." This is actually more a sense of accomplishment than an emotional or physical sensation. It doesn't raise your body temperature.

This kind of satisfaction is based on a demonstration of your skill, whether it is technical or interpersonal. You see and recognize the results, which are concrete. No one has to stroke you or point out that you have done well. Your recognition of your own competence is entirely self-generated.

If someone does tell you that you performed outstandingly well, it's frosting. You have baked the cake yourself. Self-satisfaction is the most powerful ego enhancer you can have because you make it yourself. You are in total control; you can make as little or as much ego balm as you need. If you can evaluate your own work accurately and with reasonable objectivity, you can give yourself emotional support on bad days or even during bad months. It's very sustaining. Traditionally, when people speak of the pleasure and satisfaction they get from a job, this is what they mean.

The second kind of satisfaction is external. You perform well in the eyes of others. "Jerry, that report was really well done," your boss says. Your own self-praise is triggered by feedback from others. You may subsequently congratulate yourself independent of that feedback, but only after others have pointed out why congratulations are in order.

Had someone else or several people not pointed out the value of what you had done you probably would not have recognized it. If you had recognized it, you might have had difficulty putting a value on it. How excited should you be? Have you misjudged your success? This type of stroking is less satisfying to the ego because you must constantly market and publicize what you do. People in need of external recognition end up courting it. In extreme examples, people change their work-styles in order to extract more praise. You must have a few people around you who feed your ego regularly, whether these people are subordinates, peers, or bosses.

The third and most important kind of satisfaction, from the view of potential career problems, is that which provides a physical and psychological high. However you define *high*, whether it's a momentary euphoria, an instant orgasm, or a rise in body temperature or blood pressure, it's an emotional and physical sensation, not an intellectual one.

To people who value feeling and physical sensation above either self-praise or the praise of others, the world of work must inevitably be one sustained, sequential disappointment. The reason for this is simple. No one event can produce exactly the same high twice. You're thrilled with the first sale, less so with the next, and so on until you reach "so what?" It takes more and different kinds of stimulation to generate the same level of euphoria, much less a higher level. If this sounds like a description of drug addiction, it should. Addiction to euphoria is the same thing without the physical deterioration. In work, the addiction leads to burnout.

You can recognize the symptoms of sensation addicts—we'll call them *feelies*—by the ways in which they describe what they do. Feelies never talk in terms of skills, accomplishments, or satisfaction; they speak in terms of blips on a psychic temperature chart.

"You wouldn't believe last Thursday. I've never *felt* so good about my work," or, "I wouldn't work anywhere or for anyone I didn't *feel* really good about." "I have to *feel* that what I do can really make a difference. It's not enough for me to just do my job well. That extra something has to be there."

Many people who get self-satisfaction from their jobs use the term I *feel* when they mean *I think*. They rarely mean physical sensation—a change in body reactions. The feelies mean exactly what they say. They want to *feel* physically and emotionally, not intellectually. That doesn't mean they aren't intelligent and thinking human beings. It's a question of the kind of response they want and need to get from their work in order to be satisfied and productive.

Feelies are generally well-educated professionals. Secretaries are the last and, sometimes it seems, the only realists; you'll find few in the feelie compound. The same is true of computer programmers and bank tellers. If they sought increasingly larger quantities of emotional stimulation from what they did, they would be burned out in a month. But climb a couple of rungs up the ladder and look at the commercial loan officers, information systems managers, public relations and advertising people, and a host of other people in service businesses; many of them are looking for the ultimate high. They are card-carrying feelies.

All of us want an occasional high out of work. Everybody looks forward to the Red Letter Day, the Big Contract, the stellar performance. For most people, the sensation is one of pride of performance and intense satisfaction. Not so the feelie. He or she is involved in and endless search for more sensation. No contract is so large that it can be anything more than a temporary blip on the psychic chart. No victory, however great, can be savored for long; it's got to be given short shrift as the feelie looks for the next challenge. This constant devaluing of the small triumphs of everyday work creates dissatisfaction and restlessness. It also creates foolhardy risk takers.

THE MAGNIFICENT OBSESSION

If feelies could be satisfied in some way or if their obsession didn't hurt their careers, they wouldn't be worth writing about. However, by 1980 the feelie syndrome has become the single largest cause of worker discontent, having surpassed such heavy contenders as burnout and boredom (*see* Chapter 8). It's also a source of unending aggravation to the people who manage feelies and those who work with and for them. There is no way of knowing what, if anything, motivates feelies. They can't be reasoned with, subtly threatened, or even encouraged. They are absorbed by an inner landscape hidden from everyone else.

Where did the feelies come from? Colleges can be held responsible for any number of vocational outrages, but not this one. Previous generations of students were told that they would have to work hard to get ahead, be political, and so on, just as the feelies were. Conventional wisdom doesn't change much. These lectures had no appreciable effect on workers attitude once in the job. Many of the people who went to work in the sixties and early seventies have the same conventional attitudes toward work that their parents had; they are looking for money, challenge, responsibility, and satisfaction.

Our research indicates that most feelies are single and between the ages of twenty-five and thirty-five. Sixty-five percent are female, 35 percent male.

Feelies concentrate on their jobs to the exclusion of every other interest. It's not that feelies work at their jobs 50 percent harder or even 5 percent harder than the nonfeelies. They don't. They produce about the same. The difference is that they are totally, *emotionally* involved with their jobs. Every success provides a physical and psychological high, every failure a psychological low. They feel their failures in the same way. This accounts for the extreme mood swings feelies experience. It's one day in heaven, the next in hell.

Feelies tend to put the best of themselves into their work, often to the detriment of any outside-of-work relationships. In fact, many single men and women report that they have no time for anything but their careers, including romantic involvement. They're telling the truth even though they may only be working an ordinary forty-hour week. To be outsider, their jobs may not be that absorbing or important; these people are not inventing wonder drugs to cure cancer or negotiating peace treaties in the Middle East. It's not that they are working at their jobs more intently, only that they are more emotionally lost in them. They think about work all the time, even though they may not act upon any of their ideas.

HOW AM I DOING?

Men report a tendency to replay each and every contact at work, good or bad. As one construction supervisor said, "I work eight hours a day. Then I go home and relive those eight hours at night. What should I have done differently? Was that really as good as I thought? Where do I go from here? Did I miss anything I should have caught? What does my boss really think of me?" It's endless.

For most feelies, sensation seeking proves to be both a false god and a career knockout. What happens is that the feelies become too difficult for bosses to deal with. They are asked to resign, are phased out, or leave. They drift from job to job, unfulfilled but continually looking for the ultimate high. Feelies are rarely fired for cause. They are productive. Only after managers have given up will they take such drastic action as dismissal for cause. Some managers even buy the concept that they have failed the feelie in some way.

You can check yourself and your peers to determine who's a feelie. The feelie's attitudes typically give him or her away through one of three responses.

1. The tendency to work at a job flat out only until one is sure that there is no more sensation to be wrung from it. At this point, there is a gradual slacking off. This may or may not be noticeable to others, especially if the feelie has been out-performing peers. In that case, the level of effort is reduced but it's unlikely that anyone will notice because the job is still being done well. The feelie's emotional curve may, but most often does not, coincide with the rhythm of the job. For instance, if the feelie is in a high during a departmental or organizational crisis, all goes well. Problems become apparent only when a feelie is all wrung out when a crisis looms. It's this unpredictability that threatens careers.

Lori started out as a bright new labor attorney ready to slay corporate dragons in the name of mistreated women everywhere. She slew her first dragon with wild enthusiasm. The overcoming of her second dragon was also a high. Five dragons later, Lori saw herself as up against a lifetime of repetition and diminished highs. As a pedigreed feelie, she missed the initial highs.

Her performance suffered because what she wanted from work could be satisfied only by an increasing intensity. Even a constant changing of cases could not provide that. She quit and got another job where she repeated the pattern. Both bosses had thought her either bored by the job or burned out by her own intensity. Each had suggested that she ease up a little. That solution, of course, could not help her. If anything, she needed more involvement and greater intensity.

2. The need for more and greater highs to generate the same level of job well-being. Like any addict, feelies must have regular dosage increases of the sensations they seek. They are rarely satisfied, nor can they get the same level of pleasure from the same or similar event twice. It's hardly politic for anyone to talk with a boss about the increasing need for new stimulation. Even a very liberal, with-it boss may find this sensation-seeking astonishing, even inexplicable.

Many feelies fail to recognize their own problem. It's expressed nonverbally so who can tell them what's wrong? Feelies who lack increasing stimulation from work do one of two things. They may change jobs every year or two. If that's not possible, they look for an increasing excitement level outside work. Outside-of-work sensation-seeking tends to be expressed in short-term, very intense relationships; hobbies violently pursued and then dropped; and a slavish fashionableness that exceeds even the level advocated by *Vogue* or *Gentlemen's Quarterly*.

3. The tendency to such single-focus emotional intensity that only one kind of stimulation can produce the desired sensation. This, the most extreme addiction, comes out most often as an excessive need for boss and peer approval. One of the things that managers of new MBA graduates (especially those from chic schools) report is the ever increasing, not decreasing, level of stroking and feedback these people demand. As an insurance executive vice president said, "I've been in this business thirty-five years. I am spending increasing amounts of time stroking people who should not need that much emotional support. It's as if I'm supposed to meet each of these people's total emotional needs. I just wish Thoreau could see the people we're getting now. Self-reliance, ha!"

At some point the manager who refuses to provide this stroking finds that he or she is stuck with a person whose performance is rapidly falling off.

Other people have reported that they have feelie peers who are so finely tuned that these feelies will give only halfhearted cooperation unless their emotional needs are fully met. It's a kind of organizational blackmail. Depending on their own needs for cooperation from feelies, peers may grudgingly give in. The worse possible situation is two feelies trying to wring each other out.

THE TWO OF YOU

The real problem is that there is no emotional distance between the human being and the worker. Anyone whose identity is solely tied to his or her work is a feelie. You don't have to be as extreme as some of the cases we've described. We call this a lack of "personal distance" between the roles a person must play and the real human being. Without personal distance, you can never be satisfied with any aspect of your life and that will spill over into your career. You will increasingly feel alienated from and have difficulty with those for whom and with whom you work. Unless you can view what you do for a living as a performance and not the measure of the real and total you, you are setting yourself up for a career knockout.

By the manager's standards, feelies are difficult employees once the problem has been discovered. Peers second this judgment. People may be tolerant of feelies who are highly productive in economic boom times. In recessions feelies are a problem, especially if a job isn't going to expand as rapidly as in the past. If a manager has to spend full-time on one or two people who must have constant feedback and constant stimulation, the rest of the team suffers. To a normal worker, the manager's behavior looks like favoritism toward those who are marginal producers or the most difficult. Whole departments can break out in resentment.

IS THIS A PICTURE OF YOU?

Are you a genuine feelie? Have you ever analyzed your own work needs to know if you fit the pattern? It's time to look in the mirror. You may have had inexplicable career problems which you charged up to office politics or personality differences. Your progress upward may be entirely dependent on your having moved from job to job, the jump/shift. You've never been anywhere long enough to really run out of emotional sensation or new experiences. You may have had a boss and peers who tolerated your needs. If so, you've never had to come to grips with your own needs, especially not in an increasingly hostile environment, e.g., a recession.

Testing Yourself

If you want to test the level of your own addiction, look at the following list. With which of these statements do you agree?

1. I prefer to change jobs every eighteen months to two years. There's no use sticking around once I've tested the limits of the job. If I'm not learning something new, if there's no excitement, I'm moving on.
2. I socialize a great deal with my coworkers.
3. Nobody really appreciates how hard I work, especially my boss.
4. In my scheme of values, work is most important. I define myself through my work. When someone says, "What do you do?" I always say, "Well, I'm really involved in/with . . ."
5. People who know me socially see me as either preoccupied or frantic, sometimes both at once.
6. I like to try whatever's new, regardless of merit. If miniskirts came back or pleated trousers made a return, I would whole-heartedly adopt the new style.
7. Left entirely alone without plans, I am bored.
8. I've spent a lot of time and money on my education and I really expect a payoff. Everything I do must have meaning; the more significance in my life, the better.
9. I never worry excessively about productivity as long as I feel good about my work.

10. I get depressed if nothing interesting is going on at the office. I hate dry spells. Sometimes I even try to create a bit of excitement.
11. Many of the people I work with are not concentrating on their work. They certainly don't think it's Number One.
12. My peers at work and the people I socialize with outside work share my values.
13. Hobbies are a waste of time. Everything I do should help my career.

If you agreed with eight or more of the items, you are definitely a feelie. If you agreed with from five to seven, you're a closet feelie who might be brought out later. Four or less and you're probably not much infected; you have maintained a reasonably healthy distance between you the human being and you the worker.

BUT WHAT'S WRONG WITH BEING A FEELIE?

If things are going well for you right now, why be concerned? The problem is that your ability to attain and sustain excitement in work to the exclusion of the other dimensions of your life depends on a boom economy. You depend on quick job changes to generate excitement. Our research indicates that if you were to stay at a job for five years, you would be fired for cause, extremely unhappy, or looking for a new job. With your current attitudes, you could not sustain a reasonable performance over that period of time nor could you hide your disillusionment.

Being a feelie is not quite the same thing as being a workaholic. Workaholics, who may never recognize themselves as such, are usually happy. Feelies define their own addiction by the ways in which they talk about work. Unless you diversify your interests and refocus at least some of your attention on other areas of your life, your career is going to suffer. Workaholics can sustain their performances because they work flat out without undue reflection and self-testing; feelies can't.

"JUST THE WAY I AM"

What happens to feelies who refuse to change? Most of the ones between thirty-five and forty years of age reported an almost chronic dissatisfaction with their careers that spilled over into their personal lives. There seemed to be no way for them to get back on track. Even the more self-accepting didn't realize that they'd done it to themselves. Using hindsight, their problems looked unavoidable to them. They knew they had career problems, but thought changing careers was the answer. They didn't realize that it was the *approach* they took to work rather than the work they chose to do that caused the problem. No career can be satisfactory to a sensation junkie. Anyone searching for nonstop sensation, whether bricklayer or doctor, is going to be disappointed. No job offers nonstop excitement regardless of the level of risk.

If you're going to do anything to refocus, you'll need to look at some of the issues. We've examined a few of the more·common ones.

Time Management

If you want to measure the depth of your own obsession, you might keep a daily calendar for two weeks. Keep track of what you're doing by fifteen-minute intervals. Count all of the time you spend *thinking* about work as well as the actual time you spend working. You may discover that while you work from eight to ten hours a day you are work-involved as much as from fourteen to sixteen hours each day—virtually every waking moment.

Be sure you continue your record keeping on the weekend. It will be interesting, and perhaps surprising to you, to see that your leisure time is absorbed in either thinking about or worrying about work. This should be your first real clue, if you're not already convinced, that you're a feelie. Don't forget, if you think about work as you play tennis, that counts as working time, not recreation time. This may seem extreme but you must see for yourself the depths of your problem.

Be honest in keeping this log. You can't control how you feel. The log is not an attempt to assign blame but a diagnostic tool. It is important that you find out how obsessed you really are. There's no point in making changes in your work or lifestyle unless the problem is a major one. This tool should help you make the diagnosis.

Personal Distance

Why is there no difference in the way you look at and talk about yourself the worker and the way you look at and talk about yourself the human being? One of the greatest career aids you can develop is an emotional distance from your work. You are not your work. Your work is a performance, which, like the performance of an actor or actress, is subject to review, criticism, and all the ups and downs inherent in playing a role. (Remember that actors who play Richard III and decide they *are* Richard III are institutionalized). Unless you can tell yourself that criticism of your work is not personal criticism but professional criticism—criticism of you the performer—you will remain subject to emotional fluctuations based on a misunderstanding of the human being versus the role.

Despite a supposedly open society, most people need at least two dimensions to their lives in order to act effectively in either one of them. By treating your work life as if it were the same as and indistinguishable from your personal life, you allow problems to spill over from one dimension to the other. Begin restoring your work equilibrium by making a conscious distinction between these two areas of your life; remind yourself of the distinction every time you tend to confuse the two. This will be difficult to do if you've always treated your personal life as inseparable from your work life. It's also the only way to put work into perspective. There are people who believe they will advance more rapidly if they are obsessed. There is no evidence to support this. The evidence suggests that what you get from single-mindedness are emotional exhaustion and burnout, not promotions.

Do They Like Me?

Feelies worry excessively about their relationships with people at work; they must genuinely like and be liked by colleagues and bosses. They see these people as potential friends. That's a mistake. The people with whom you work can never be friends in the same way that people who are permanent non-competitors can be. Anyone with whom or for whom you work or who is involved in the politics of your workplace can't be a friend. Friendships will not flourish in that environment and you shouldn't try to force them to do so. There's always some degree of wariness between people who may be on opposite sides and fighting for their careers at any time.

New Interests

How can you generate new activities that give you a healthy satisfaction? Two methods have worked with a significant number of people: 1) return to school in an area unrelated to your work and 2) get involved with a cause unrelated to your work. Sometime, long ago and far away, before you became a feelie, you had other interests. Dredge up one of those or find a new one. Don't seduce yourself with the idea that becoming a more active participant in your trade or professional association will give you a different perspective. That's something you should do throughout your career, but as part of your work, not personal, life.

The new activity you adopt should be a noncompetitive one. You shouldn't care whether you are the most outstanding student or performer. You are going to try to learn how internal work satisfaction is generated. The results of your activity should be concrete. If you decide to study art history, you should be able to see that you know measurably more about a particular period of school art after completing the course. Craft or hobby activities should produce something tangible: stamps stuck in books; photographs taken and developed; needlepoint pillows lording it over the sofa cushions; books read.

Some feelies, having recognized the symptoms, will decide on professional counseling as an aid to help provide them with a fresh perspective. The feelie syndrome is a fairly common problem these days; it does not usually require six years of analysis to make a dent in it. If counseling is your choice, be sure you get some references on the counselor you choose before you get involved—financially and emotionally. Don't jump into a full-blown program only to discover three months later that it's not the right one for you, that the approach to the problem is wrong for you. Talk to friends who have also had work-satisfaction problems. Find out who or what helped them. People who've recovered, like the members of Alcoholics Anonymous, are a source of assistance to fellow sufferers. Find them and get help.

Personal Networks

How many and what kinds of people are there in your personal as opposed to your professional network? When you count up the number of people you regularly see, how many names come to mind? If all of your friends are people you work with or have worked with in the past, you essentially rely on competitors—potential or past—for emotional support. This will always be a less secure source of support because the network lacks the stability of undivided interest. If you are seeking friendship through work, it puts those people and you in a double bind. As we said, if the competition heats up and you have to act in your own self-interest, it could leave you bereft of friends at a time when you will need them most. One way to reduce your dependence on work for emotional fulfillment is to increase the number and variety of your contacts who are wholly divorced from your work.

Since you are primarily work-centered, try non-work-related associations: butterfly fanciers or bird-watchers or ecologists. Presumably these people will not share your particular work interest, nor will they be competitors. Look to college or high school alumni groups for contacts. Why shouldn't people you enjoyed in the past be brought back into your network? In your obsession, you may have lost touch. The community of interests you still share with many of these people will amaze you.

Thirty-Minute Breaks

The hardest sale to make to die-hard feelies is to convince them that every minute of the day need not be divided between work and self-improvement. You can lessen your own work involvement by allocating thirty minutes a day to an activity that will not improve you in any way. Some people call this relaxing. This automatically excludes exercise. What is it for except to improve you? Reading self-help books is work. Only trashy novels and worthless movies guaranteed to raise your libido and lower your intellect qualify. Other purely escapist sources must be similarly unproductive.

This means you may have to spend considerable time thinking of an activity. Television, a confirmed mind rotter, might be good. A serious feelie is always appalled by the notion that there is any good to be derived from watching television unless it is a program on public television or one related to news. Still, it is not high on the list of activities promising self-improvement. If you really do develop other interests that help reestablish a more healthy relationship between you and your work, you can then go back to a cautious program of self-improvement. You can't go back to self-improvement nonstop, however, or you'll have to go through the whole process again.

Don't give up. You may still have periods when you want, or feel you must have, an increasing emotional high from your job. You're not going to crack this addiction in three days or even in three months. Begin by evaluating your own work and by giving yourself credit for what you do well. Do this even if you have to talk out loud to yourself in front of the bathroom mirror. (Close the door if you have a roommate.) You'll be well down the road to recovery when you get as much satisfaction from self-praise as from the praise of others. That's the real message. Self-satisfaction is the other high that lasts and cannot be diminished by outsiders. Best of all, you can recreate the satisfaction of a good or great performance anytime by conjuring up the scene in your mind; you are an actor replaying a role. You'll be more productive and more satisfied.

Chapter 4
Skills Failures, Assessment, and the Road Back

Failing at office politics can certainly be a career knockout. You're going to bleed because you didn't fit in and couldn't please the boss. There's one kind of failure that's worse, however, and that's a skills failure. It's a nightmare because it shatters both your personal and your professional ego. You may be demoted, transferred, asked to resign, or fired outright because you can't do your job. You do not have the technical skills, perhaps not even the basic knowledge, needed to do what you are being paid to do. This is one of the bitterest pieces of information a worker can be asked to ingest. It's especially dispiriting to learn of this inability to do the job the ultimate hard way—by being fired. This produces stress and anxiety, and can result in a long-term crisis of self-confidence. Although it can happen to anyone at any age, younger workers seem to be most susceptible. In business downturns, during cutbacks and reorganizations, it happens more frequently as bosses look at worker productivity with a highly critical eye.

Skills failure is the ultimate career knockout because being identified as a skills failure tells you that you are incompetent in some way. Incompetence is the bottom line. You can be skilled at office politics, charismatic, beloved by clients, cooperative, a team player, bright, well educated with a degree or degrees from a good school, and adored by your boss and peers. None of these will save your job nor make up for your inability to do it. In every job, sooner or later there comes a time when you must put a finished piece of work on your boss's desk for judgment. He or she is then going to decide how well that work has been done. Is it acceptable? If he or she decides that your work is not acceptable (however defined), the boss must face the critical questions: Can you do the work? Do you have the necessary skills? Are you simply unable to do what is wanted.

THE SETUP

Here's what often happens to people with skills deficiencies. You have taken a job which both you and the prospective boss agree you should be able to do. You'll have to stretch a little but that's the challenge everyone thinks is so important for professional growth. You are assured that you will get some on-the-job training. Not only are you going to make a decent salary, you are also going to be upgrading your skills and acquiring new ones. You are on the road to genuine career advancement.

One month goes by and you find yourself in a very uncertain position. The job is indeed as described but the training you had been promised has not materialized. You are supposed to be able to do things that you have never learned to do. You keep asking questions about those tasks and you get very specific, limited answers. You work harder or at least you think you do.

Going Under

At the end of the second month, your boss gives you an informal performance appraisal. You are not "taking hold" as expected. "I really have high hopes for you," the boss says. You somewhat reluctantly mention your need for training. The boss agrees that there had been talk of training when you were hired but the seven other employees who had the job before you all managed to "pick things up." You are sunk. Those seven former employees are an unmistakable clue that the situation is desperate, probably terminal.

In some cases, you may have heard a predecessor or two criticized as a slow learner. You had thought no one could be a quicker study than you. Hadn't you done really well in school and on other jobs?

You begin to develop a genuine sympathy for those past job twins.

Your boss, whatever is said, never trained any of your predecessors either. They all went through what you're going through now or at least one or two fewer alumni would have gotten the "wonderful opportunity" presented to you. Suddenly you are face-to-face with the fact that your job is in mortal danger. Things are not going to improve. Somehow you must train yourself in skills you may not even know you need. You keep plugging away, hoping for a miracle.

The Last Roundup

Two months later comes the Last Conference. Your boss comes into your office or calls you into his or hers. It's Friday at 4:30 P.M. and you are asked to close the door. You know what is coming. After the usual pleasantries and throat clearing, the boss asks you to resign. The boss does not acknowledge that you were set up. He or she admits no role in your downfall. You have been *a disappointment*. You simply haven't the skills necessary to do the job. You haven't been able to pick up enough expertise in four months. There is no one with the time, or it seems the desire, to train you. It would be better all around if you left. Of course, the boss likes you very much; all of the people in the company like you. You are a certifiably nice, bright person. Still, you can't do the job—you are not competent. That is that.

You get one month's severance pay even though you've only been there four months. This is a sure sign that your boss feels guilty. You get a glowing letter of recommendation. It states that your job was eliminated or restructured. You are asked to write a similarly glowing letter of resignation telling them how sorry you are to depart. You get a free lunch with the boss at a restaurant to which heartburn victims go for rehabilitation, and, if female, you get to keep the spider plant that decorated your office. You leave.

This has been a humane way to get rid of you. The boss could have fired you for incompetence sans severance pay and letter of recommendation just as easily. There have been cases in which the boss did everything possible to put the entire blame for a skills failure on the worker, a corporate version of *The Bad Seed*.

FACING A SKILLS FAILURE

You will never have to face a tougher situation. It's a genuine career crisis. You have failed not politically, not interpersonally, not because you had a fatal flaw; you have failed because you have a skills deficiency. The knowledge that somehow you were not as qualified as you thought—and as your employer hoped—is not just a career setback, it is a potential career killer. At the least, your confidence is likely to be temporarily shattered.

Unless you have spent all of your previous working life in a cloistered religious order, you are aware that many apparently wholly incompetent or partially incompetent people are working regularly. Some do get fired with some frequency but their views of themselves are such that they get new jobs and carry on their careers with a minimum of difficulty. A professional incompetent must have superb selling skills in order to survive. Developing such selling skills is almost more difficult than becoming competent in some way in the first place.

Actors frequently face this problem. In one movie, a performer gets rave reviews. In the next, the same performer is called "wooden," "unconvincing," and "technically unassured." In other words, in that place and in that role the actor or actress is incompetent. Your situation is similar even if you are thinking in terms of an entire career and not just one role. No one's career can be judged all of a piece until after retirement.

TRAINING FAILURE OR SKILLS FAILURE?

Like any successful performer you must learn to do your own skills assessment. It may be true that you lacked certain skills essential to the job. You definitely lacked them in a sufficient quantity or quality to meet your boss's expectations. If you needed training and did not get it, you simply got in over your head. Strictly speaking your skills problems were correctable had you been given the needed training; they are still correctable. That much has not changed. Setting people up for failure by letting them get into situations they haven't the skills and experience to handle doesn't bother every employer. It's still aggressively unreasonable to expect someone to pick up hard techniques out of the air as if he or she were a sponge or a human air fern. If you are ever in such a spot again, you will quickly recognize that without real training you can't possibly develop the skills you must have on the job.

Few people can remain unshaken by being fired because they couldn't do the job, however impossible the odds for success seemed in looking back. Many people have doubts about how well they can do any new job. They assume that "they" wouldn't put them in the job if "they" didn't think they could do it. Sometimes the person who made this assumption is right, sometimes wrong.

Assess or Fail

You have two choices. You can learn to more accurately assess your skills before you take a job or you can rely on your prospective employer to do so. You've already seen some of the problems inherent in the latter choice. It's what got you into trouble in the first place. You must learn to measure your competence for any particular task independent of anyone else's assessment. You must be able to assess with reasonable accuracy the skills any person would need to do the job. Then you've got to be able to judge, usually without much hard evidence, whether your skills match what's needed to do the job.

Most people put a tremendous amount of effort into improving their human relations skills. But, except when actively job hunting, they seldom reassess the level of technical skills they have nor do they compare these with the skills other people doing the same job might possess. It's not easy to measure how much you know about how to do something unless it's something that can only be done one way. For instance, if you're building a cabinet according to a set of plans, you can see step-by-step the tasks you must be able to do to make the thing fit together if you are to end up with a usable piece of furniture. When you're supervising seven people under intense pressure to get the work out, there is no blueprint. You won't even know if you put the tasks together properly until someone sees the final project and says it's okay.

More Skill or Less?

How do you measure skills that don't come with operating instructions? First, a skill is a competency. For instance, speaking in whole sentences is a skill. You learned how to do it. The major property of a skill, whatever it's called, is that it is learned. The skills you want to measure and those needed to do a particular task. A task is the use of a series of skills. Many tasks together form a job.

There are two principal methods for measuring skills. The first is to look at the output you want to achieve and then try to work back from there. This means taking apart the finished product and decoding what you have to know in order to asemble it in the first place.

The second method is to watch someone who's doing the task with reasonable success and see what motions he or she goes through. This, by the way, is one of the genuine benefits of student internship programs and harks back to the time-honored apprenticeship programs of highly skilled craftsmen. If there is anything that may help college students today avoid potential skills failures after graduation, it's internship program and co-op programs. Under co-op programs, students in technical areas such as engineering and accounting work a quarter or semester full-time for a company and attend classes for another quarter or semester. It takes longer to get a degree this way, but, in addition to salary, co-op programs provide excellent on-the-job training. Many students end up working for the organizations with which they interned.

Skills other than those used in technical areas respond to intensive observation. The value of watching a competent professional go through the motions of any particular job can hardly be overestimated. If the task involves extensive reasoning and a series of choices, you'll have to get the person you're watching talking about what he or she is thinking and how he or she makes certain decisions. For example, why is a particular memo organized the way it is? The first paragraph is good news, the middle paragraph gives the bad news, and the last paragraph is good news again. Does such a strategy get better results? What other strategy might work if you didn't have enough good news to wrap around the bad news?

Knowing vs. Doing

It's always a mistake to assume that having studied a subject in school somehow qualifies or equips you to put that knowledge to work on a job. Some subjects do lend themselves more to practice. Accounting, nursing, and newspaper reporting come to mind. Still, there is extensive on-the-job training in these fields.

Many people suffer from the liberal arts syndrome. What can an English major *do* versus what does an English major *know*? There is an enormous difference between knowing the theory and having developed the skills to apply the theory. There are techniques to literary criticism, editing, and writing for publication that are rarely taught in literature courses. The study of a body of knowledge implies no skill except a skill in studying. If you confuse the skills needed to study and learn with the skills needed to do something with the knowledge you've amassed, you are suffering from acute intellectual arrogance. You also have no understanding of the differences between knowing and doing.

Training vs. Theory

The need for training should never be confused with the need for a theoretical base. Going to seminars in business writing three times a week will not help you learn to write as much as would thirty minutes a day of critique from a professional. Someone who says, "Move this paragraph. This isn't the right word. Beef this up. You need more facts here," is providing training, not just theory. It's invaluable. Unless you find someone to help you in that way, you are slowed down as you try to learn on your own by trial and error. It's worth it, particularly if you are changing careers or just beginning a career, to search carefully for a hands-on trainer who both enjoys teaching and giving feedback and who has the time and intent to do so.

MANAGEMENT MYOPIA

Remember that people who expect new employees to pick things up on their own may have a variety of other management problems. Managers who can't or won't give specific instructions and then feedback as you attempt to follow them are setting you up for failure. Some honestly believe that you can be trained only through trial and error. There can be only one result. Unless you got your B.A. in mind reading with a minor in osmosis, you don't have a chance.

Beware of people who can't tell you why something doesn't or can't work, whether it's a program, an idea, or a formula. If someone doesn't know why something isn't a good idea or physically won't work and can't suggest diagnostic techniques you can use, you're working for someone with a degree from the Mystical Magic School of Management. Management by divine relation can hamper your ability to learn anything, not to mention what it will do to your confidence in yourself; destroy it completely, for instance.

Beware of all people who urge you to "trust" them. Of course, some mutual trust is essential; it's blind trust that gets people into trouble. Trust is no substitute for technique backed up by hard knowledge and logic. Everybody needs to know the theory that is supposed to support what they are trying to do. Anyone who wants you to trust them rather than take the time to explain why something must be done a certain way is never going to give you enough training to make you either competent or independent. This may be deliberate. Someone wants to keep you checking back. It may simply be a style of management with overtones of power retention.

YOUTH AND LACK OF EXPERIENCE

The two groups of workers most likely to have skills failures and consequent skills assessment problems are workers with a total of less than five years of job experience and women returning to work after an absence of from ten to twenty years. Both will have crises of confidence as they try desperately to assess what they're expected to do and then do it. It's not much comfort, but some of the learning can only be gotten through trial and error. A job has to provide a climate in which errors can be tolerated and then corrected. Absolute skills assessment will always be easier if done on yourself by yourself.

The most difficult task is assessing the skills a job requires. Don't ever be misled by job descriptions. Unless you're applying for a job as a typist or bricklayer, where you are expected to produce at a given rate per minute or hour, job descriptions are more like topic outlines than like road maps.

Back on the Horse

Despite your job failure and advice from your ten closest friends to choose a new career, you have decided that what you were trying to do is still what you want to do. You liked it very much and you are determined to hone your skills until you can do the job and do it well. Let's assume that the job was manager of a sales department. Of course, you can always return to sales in another organization. How do you decide what skills you actually need? Where do you get the needed training and feedback without jeopardizing your career?

There are four principal ways of finding out what skills are needed for a particular job or kind of job. Depending on your needs and your time frame, you may want to use one or all four.

1. **Through your contacts, identify the top working professionals who do that job and talk to them.** Who are the acknowledged veterans in your business? Call the president or membership chairperson of your trade association and ask for help in identifying these people. Once you've got the names, track them down and make appointments to see them, either in their offices or at association meetings. Prepare a list of specific questions you plan to ask. You're likely to get meaningless generalities if you simply ask what's necessary for success. You'll know you're on the right track in questioning people if your questions start with "how" or "how much." "How much does writing count in sales promotion?" "How is that writing different from the kind done in public relations agencies?" If you were talking about public accounting versus private company accounting, you could ask, "How much of your time is spent on financial reporting, governmental reports, or work with auditors versus cost accounting? How does dealing with top management differ from dealing with clients?"

You'll need to talk to at least ten people and you'll have to take very good notes. Concentrate on the areas your boss identified as your weakest or on the tasks you couldn't do at all.

2. **Identify any academic weaknesses you may have.** You simply could not prepare a decent budget even though your boss tried to explain the process to you on several occasions. Your nearest community

college or business school either has or can recommend a course on accounting for nonaccountants. If the community college has such a course and the term is already under way, contact the instructor for some private tutoring. Many people who teach courses at community colleges are eager to make such arrangements, for a price of course.

You couldn't write a decent memo. A workshop with a professional who sits down with you and goes over and over the same techniques can move you a long way toward competence.

3. Get involved as a volunteer by doing for some organization what you were supposed to do on your job. People for whom you are working for free have a tremendous incentive to train you. Anything you don't do they may end up doing personally. Make sure the person who is training you is a competent professional. Learning from an also-ran may be worse than not learning at all.

4. Get a job one rung lower on the ladder than the one you had and with an organization that does have on-the-job training. What is your career worth to you? If you think that anything but a straight shot to the top is worthless, you're mistaken. Few people are going to know or care that you've changed to a lesser job. Don't enlighten them. You are trying to play catch-up with your career. If you have a deficiency, you really can't correct it too quickly. Thorough training now will help you leapfrog over competitors later.

Organizational Diagnosis

How can you find out what skills are really needed to do a particular job before you're trying to do it and sinking rapidly? Step one is always to make sure you don't rush through the interview process, especially the part during which you are supposed to ask specific questions. Some of the questions you'll want to ask—especially if you're gun shy after a skills failure—include: 1) How much experience did my predecessor have when you hired him or her? 2) What is the most important, time-consuming, or essential part of the job? 3) Why did my predecessor leave? 4) What kind of training do you provide for this job? How much time does this usually take? 5) How long do I have to learn the job? 6) On what will my performance appraisal be based? 7) What's most important in evaluating my work? 8) How many people have had this job in the past five years? You get the drift. Be sure to include questions that thoroughly cover the skills failure you experienced.

Even if you have to stall during the interview process to do so, try to find the person who had the job before you and talk to him or her. The extra effort to do this will be well worthwhile. In our original example, the fact that seven other people had already drowned in that particular pool should have discouraged the latest swimmer; it probably would have had it been known. In retrospect, extreme caution was obviously called for. It is always up to the job hunter to find out things like this. What boss would offer such information, especially if he or she were beginning to see a pattern and, instead of correcting his or her own managerial deficiencies, kept hoping for a miracle? Mystical Magic School of Management graduates do a lot of hoping.

If you talk to your predecessor, you may learn that you are not likely to be able to do the job or you could learn that it won't be a problem at all! It's amazing how little value bosses place on this comparison process, to their own eventual injury and cost. Time spent comparing those who've done well in a job with new applicants would be time well spent. If you can't turn up a predecessor, try for someone doing the same job in a competitor's shop. Personality differences are important, of course, so there is no exact comparison. However, if the supposed job twin has vastly different skills and talks about tasks that use those skills you'll know you're not on particularly firm ground.

Talk to people who have moved up from that particular job—in the organization you're interested in or others. What, in retrospect, seems to them to have been critical to success or failure? Don't be surprised if their perspective is vastly different from that of your immediate predecessor in the job. Both views are important; they help you assemble the truth from fragments of evidence.

The amount of trust people place in people they don't know and the amount of control they give up over their own careers as a consequence is insane. You are the person who will pay the price for blind, unjustified faith. If you have had one skills failure, no amount of effort, research, or time put into securing the next position will be wasted. A second skills failure would be even more devastating emotionally than the first. The power of positive thinking will be taxed in talking yourself "up" at that point. Perhaps you are entitled, or even prone, to one skills failure if you're very young, but who wants one? Prevention is a much better strategy.

Second Time Around

If you are a woman returning to work after a long period of working at home, you have a special problem. It will take time to verify for yourself that everybody who's working near you and who's fifteen years younger is not necessarily either brighter or more skilled. In our work with second-time beginners, a great many express fear of getting into situations they won't have the skills to handle. They are significantly more concerned about this problem than they are about starting too far down the career ladder. The returnee can develop no more important skill than the ability to analyze her own level of skill at any particular task. Taking a job because you need the money and the salary is right is an even higher risk if you are a returnee than it is for a twenty-two-year old. You need to make the right start, build your skills, and move ahead as quickly as you can. One or more skills failures would slow you down drastically; you don't have that much time to waste.

AFTERSHOCKS

After a skills failure, emotional pain and recurring bouts of self-doubt are to be expected; once planted, the doubt about your competence is more difficult to uproot than a dandelion with a twenty-inch taproot. Every time you think you've exorcised the doubt and pain, a feeling that escaped capture turns up to bother you. Don't dwell on the way you feel.

If you learn only one thing from your experience, learn that the only way to survive in any work situation is to see yourself as a performer trying to play a particular role. Never insist on seeing yourself as incompetent; if you do, you're through. Without extensive therapy, you cannot recover from the kind of ego devastation caused by such a self-portrait. Focus on the knowledge that your performance was not completely or fully competent at one time and in one place. It's what you tell yourself about the relationship between you the human being and you the performer in the roles you play that determines how quickly you'll rebound.

If your boss added humiliation and personal rancor, "I took a chance on you and you let me down," to the pain of a skills failure, it will take longer to recover. Repeat this thought ten times a day until the pain diminishes. "Everybody who hires anybody takes a chance that the person may fail as well as succeed. By taking the job, the employee takes the same chance and has every right to say, 'I took a chance on *you,* the boss, as well. *You* also let me down.'" If you don't think this is true, ask others with whom or for whom you work what they think. You are used to thinking that bosses hold all the aces and that you're a victim. That attitude won't help you as you try to restructure your career for greater success.

Many people who've had a skills failure respond by accepting the boss's judgment and trying to sweep the whole episode under the carpet. "Yes, I am incompetent. What I need is to return to school and train for a whole new career—another new beginning. I will pretend this never happened and I will simply choose something new." Such an approach rarely works, especially if your skills failure was one of lack of experience and technique rather than theory. Schools teach theory in a great many fields; they rarely provide knowledge that is tranferable, as is, to a job. By training for a new career without doing the appropriate postmortem on the old, you are setting yourself up to repeat the experience. We've worked with people who have enough different degrees to qualify them as major cash donors to universities. The degrees mean nothing unless they are accompanied by the training to turn "knowing" into "doing."

Some people make another mistake. The worst possible time to pick a new career is immediately following a skills failure. At this time you're twice as likely to make a bad choice based on emotion as you would be were you sitting in a job you'd mastered and thinking logically about your next move. "I can't seem to manage people; therefore I'll become an engineer and work with ideas and things." The either/or approach means that you're going from one extreme to another. How do you know that engineers with highly technical expertise don't have to manage people? (They frequently do.) Is there any career for which you can train that will be completely free of people problems? (Not that we know of, but if you find one please call us collect.) Even entrepreneurs, artists, writers, and inventors have people with whom they must work, people who judge them and their work. You'll be light-years ahead if you focus on picking up the pieces and testing your skills and improving them. Pick a new career only after you've done this, and then only if it seems best. Don't act out a sense of panic, because you see yourself as a failure who must "start over."

Don't spend a great deal of your time and emotional energy focusing on the fact that everybody on your job liked you despite your lack of skill. Look-

97

ing for some bright spot in an otherwise depressing terrain, a great many people clutch at the fact that they have highly developed social skills. These skills are irrelevant now. Why focus on them at the expense to you in the long run?

Don't look to anyone but your immediate family and intimate friends for comfort. Any kind of failure makes people uneasy, especially your business colleagues or casual acquaintances. If, as in our original example, the organization gave you a perfect out when it said your job had been eliminated, don't undermine the story. If you do, your former boss may get wind of it and feel that there's no longer a reason not to give out the true explanation. You don't need that. If you have a reference problem, see Chapter 6, "The Bad Reference," for help.

You have an opportunity, even if it's one you didn't seek out, to improve your skills. Would you prefer a skills failure twenty years from now? How would you feel if you were fired after twenty years on the job and told that the company had carried you all those years? That your boss thought you'd never really been a competent, productive employee? This is the awful alternative some people have had to face.

As one recovered "victim" said, "I will never again be as casual, either in looking at myself or at a prospective job. It took me about a year to fully recover my self-confidence. Every time a piece of work was criticized in my new job I would cringe and wonder what was coming. What has been my salvation has been the development of some skill in self-criticism. I now have a pretty good idea of the quality of the work I do."

Chapter 5
Job Hopping

"How long do you plan to stay with this job?"

"Are you looking for something permanent?"

"How long were you on your last job?"

"Why did you leave such a good job? You were making more than we could afford to pay you."

These questions occur in almost every initial interview, whether it be with a personnel specialist or the manager who may hire you. Usually they signal the fact that you're talking to somebody who's been burned by a job hopper and thinks he or she recognizes you as a member of the club.

"My God," the vice president said, "how could he possibly know if he even liked the job, much less whether there was any room to move up? He was only here nine months. He'd barely learned what we expected him to do. He hadn't even been permanently assigned to an office."

Said another, "That's the second time I've been burned by somebody who looked good but had a résumé with a lot of short-term jobs. I'm not ever going to interview anyone again who hasn't been on his present job at least three years."

Victims Left Behind

Personnel people, line managers, and workers hired to replace them agree that job hoppers should be on everybody's hit list. Job hoppers are the industrial society's version of itinerant peddlers. They leave behind wary employers and successors who'll have to stay longer just to get a decent reference.

Technically, job hoppers come in two varieties. 1) People who make many job changes within the same field over a fairly long period of time, generally keeping the same title and amount of responsibility. Job hoppers who have moved up each time or more often than not are still job hoppers; they're "fast track" job hoppers. Seven to ten jobs in five years, one or two of which were three- to six-month engagements, is the classic pattern. It's the one most managers and personnel people have in mind when they use the term. 2) People who change the kind of work they do each time they change employers. These people could be called career hoppers rather than job hoppers, but to an employer this appears to be more or less the same thing. Many of the second type will start in one field at entry level, move to an entry-level job in a different field, and then to another and another.

Despite all of the media attention to career change, it is still met with skepticism and resistance in many businesses simply because it is a change. Career changers exude a faint but unmistakable aura of indecision. Even though life can't be made to fit a hypothetical model, many personnel people and managers prefer the good old days of employees whose only concern was job security. These people went to work for a company as soon as they got out of school and stayed until they died of boredom or retired. There were never as many of these people as supposed. But even a few seemed an organizational blessing in an era of increasing worker mobility.

Job hopping has an age dimension. If personnel people had a choice (if unable to screen out the hoppers entirely), they'd prefer that all job hopping be done by people under twenty-five or no more than thirty. This would then be the corporate version of "sowing wild oats," tolerable if not explicable. Then, having had a period of frivolity, the person would become a serious, committed worker and settle down to work until death or retirement.

As the economy sickens and the energy crisis deepens, a great many people face involuntary job change through organizational cutbacks. They look like job hoppers even though they really aren't. These people are victims. Generally the large number of jobs they've had in a given period of time can be explained to the satisfaction of even the most conservative employer. This is the case even though, to look at the individual's résumé, you'd think you were seeing one of that dreaded species, the job hopper.

STABLE, THEN FRANTIC

Job hoppers don't start out with job hopping as a primary career goal. Typically, according to our research, each stays at the first and second jobs for from two to four years. There was no sign during those first two jobs that this person was about to embark on a new work pattern. Many had glowing references from their first and second jobs, even invitations to return. They seemed productive and well regarded. They also appeared to have been reasonably satisfied at those jobs.

Then came a series of four, five, or even ten short-term (less than one year) jobs. The person changed his or her work-style at about age twenty-eight; some began to change as late as thirty-five, ordinarily men. They are the late bloomers of job hopping.

Frequent job changes appear to fill a need to experiment. Sometimes it signals a real indecisiveness about the direction in which an individual wants to go. This indecision is not the same thing as having made a wrong job choice. Job hoppers display a restlessness, an impatience, almost a visceral need to move. For them, at a certain period of their lives, there is no *one* right job. They seem to need to be on site and working in an organization before they can determine whether or not it is a satisfactory connection.

WHAT HO, SWEET PRINCE

For women, job hopping is often a response to the dawning realization that The Prince is not, as expected, going to appear on cue. In fact, there may be growing doubts as to the existence of The Prince. The Prince may have arrived and then departed. Even in the 1980s, a great many bright, educated, otherwise ambitious and career-oriented women put off major career decisions until they've met The Prince and gotten married, presumably so that he can "share" her life decisions.

"I didn't begin to think seriously about law school or getting a better job in my present company until my twenty-seventh birthday," Ellen said. "After all, what if I met someone who wanted to move to another state? It would have meant lots of conflicts and rearranging my life. Once I realized I was really the only one in charge of me, I began to make all kinds of decisions. I developed a real direction for my life."

Once that assumption of how life ought to work out is in doubt, women particularly come back to reality with a thump. There is an increased awareness that they may be self-supporting indefinitely. This always raises doubts about previous career decisions. Is what they are doing now the best choice? What other options should be considered? Is this the time to make a major change? As one woman said, "If work is really going to be a permanent part of my life, it's going to be the most interesting, rewarding work I can find."

NO FREE LUNCH

For men, the early thirties are critical. Many we talked to had been sure that the organization they worked for had career paths, one of which they'd follow onward and upward. Armed with MBAs and other appropriate degrees, they found not career paths but political thickets full of twisted paths and misread signs. This caused them to question the "corporation-will-provide" assumption. One reorganization or merger will make a nonbeliever out of the most starry-eyed idealist.

The next question was, "What am I going to do for myself to protect my own interests?" Despite nonworking wives and small children, disillusionment made job hoppers out of the most prudent men. With a working spouse, the decision to move around more often was no problem at all.

PROMISES, PROMISES

It's not the organization's frustration (that's what personnel people are paid to worry about) but the potential long-term damage to the individual job hopper's career that concerns us. Many job hoppers develop premature regrets about having moved so often because they don't know the facts. They don't realize that there are ways to move without permanent or even temporary career damage.

There are many ways in which job hoppers can move with grace. For example, you take a job in good faith sans promises to stay forever. (It's foolish to promise that anyway.) You perform well but leave after three to six months without having made any to-the-death enemies. There are two possible outcomes: 1) your reference from that organization will be compromised because the person giving it feels deceived and/or 2) you will be able to slip out relatively unscathed because you were not there long enough to cause any severe problems for the people for whom you worked.

You sold yourself in the interview as a conservative, sober, promotable employee. The prospective employer congratulated himself because he thought he was getting just what he'd always wanted. His days of interviewing were at an end. You depart leaving the employer bruised and angry. He had spent three months training you and now both you and the money are gone. Your reference will be unfavorable no matter what anyone in the personnel department tells you.

You took a job that wasn't that great to begin with. You then proceeded to poison the atmosphere with your verbal and nonverbal complaints. The salary was too low. The job had no content or real responsibility. (Real responsibility is an interesting idea because any responsibility is real.) Your boss is glad to see you depart and may even wish you well. Your reference will not be good and will characterize you as "uncooperative" or even as a "troublemaker."

The hidden killer in job hopping, even as you get different or better jobs, is what drifting can do to your references and your ability to get good ones. No manager, however inattentive or presold on you, can fail to pick up the fact that you're a job hopper when reading your application. The more short-term jobs you show, the more carefully your references will be checked. Nobody views this as a situation of restlessness or indecisiveness. Managers expect the worst. You must have done something to irritate somebody, even if it appears you left voluntarily.

"We recommend . . ."

Anyone who job hops has got to secure his or her flanks before moving on by making sure that a decent reference will be available from someone in authority in the organization. That means that slipping away on short notice will be almost impossible. Of course, if you only look like a job hopper because two jobs in a row were reorganized out of existence before you'd been there long enough to locate the health insurance forms, you will probably find the hiring company sympathetic about references. The same is true if some of your references are from companies that have since gone under. This is especially so if you explain that such involuntary departure has several times been your fate.

If, however, you have left several jobs in a row with marginal references because you irritated people with broken promises and quick departures, you've got a potential career knockout. That's a hidden danger. It'll be more and more difficult to sell an employer on the idea that you've finally decided what you want as you have more and more jobs behind you.

Telling job hoppers to stay put somewhere for a few years is silly. Job hopping is not a style most of them see themselves as having chosen. It just happens, or it's something they feel they must do. If they have good contacts who feed them job leads, the reference issue may not come up for five or ten years. They are essentially coming to the interview with the new organization with someone's blessing. Nobody thinks to question what the last boss or the last organization thought about the person's departure unless burned by previous hoppers. It may not even be known that the person moves frequently. He or she does an excellent job of selling skills and using contacts.

Headhunters Beware

The pattern of job hopping can continue without any discernible damage to one's career as long as the person never has to job hunt through personnel departments, headhunters, or personnel agencies. Once forced back on these resources, the damage comes to light. These groups do check references and they are often very concerned with how long someone has stayed at a particular job. Some search firms won't even talk to people who've moved more than three times in five years. Their disapproval of the job hopper is hardly an ethical one. It's a gut feeling of unease combined with experience that the job they have to offer may not break the streak. In the case of headhunters and personnel agencies, that means no fee and an angry client. Why take the risk?

Job hopping in the 1980s will be a particular problem. Job hoppers will be seen as individuals too hungry for advancement or too picky to be pleased for very long and as a waste of scarce resources—time and training. If an organization is searching for ways to stabilize its work force, it will want to minimize risk by avoiding hoppers.

If you fit the job hopper's profile, what do you do? Especially if you're now in a job that you want to leave, or may soon be asked to leave? You need to do some serious planning before you make any moves. You must intensively analyze your skills and goals and make a realistic appraisal of you prospects. If you don't, you are asking for a long period of unemployment or unrealistically counting on prospects not checking your references. This is always a high-risk assumption. Managers have instincts about people that they go with.

Some problems can be easily masked, but poor or even hostile references are not among them. Some of your former bosses, still angry at your departure, may even voluntarily call a prospective employer and, unknown to you, ruin the opportunity. Remember that both the "old boy" and "new girl" networks are alive and functioning.

Of course, if you've kept up your contacts with trade and professional associations, maintained a high visibility with peers in the field, or work in a field where people are traditionally gypsies, your problem is not as acute.

Overripe Banana!

If you're over forty and spent your thirties flitting, your problem will be compounded by hidden age discrimination. It's no particular revelation to point out that what's brave and idealistic in a twenty-seven-year-old looks overripe in someone fifteen years older. Employers have many age-related assumptions, which, while they often bear no resemblance to the facts, are acted upon nonetheless. "Carefree," "happy-go-lucky," and "experimental" turn into "unstable," "indecisive," and "poor risk" over the years.

THE ROAD BACK

All of this is not particularly helpful if you're currently unemployed with a résumé that shows you've been through enough jobs to allow an employment agency owner to winter on the Riviera with fees collected from your moves. It does mean that you're going to have to take certain steps if you're to move back into the mainstream. First, you will have to do enough work and make enough hard decisions to develop a profile of a job with which you can live for several years. With as much experience as you have and as many different environments as you've tried, this should be possible although it may be tedious. Determine what you've liked in the past and try to develop an outline for the future. Second, you will have to use contacts or develop contacts you can use instead of personnel people or agencies. Otherwise you are going to be screened out at every step.

Third, you need a functional résumé, one that doesn't show a chronology of your life and require five detailed pages to do so. Reorganize your résumé on a skills basis and showcase your successes. It won't keep people from asking where you worked specifically and for how long but, if you're selling yourself well enough, it may soften some of the negative vibrations that could come your way.

Fourth, you are going to have to check your own references and see what people are saying about you. This is essential. You can kill off a really good prospect if the reference check is negative. Whatever method you decide to use to check on what your past employers are saying, it must be done. The easiest way is probably to get someone in a business to call and ask if you worked at the company and if your work was satisfactory. If the reply is negative, you'll have to do one of two things.

You cannot really convince people to avoid checking references by saying that you had a "personality conflict" or some such thing with your boss. That only makes people want to check more carefully. You can rarely get away with the explanation that your boss is no longer there and you don't know where he or she has gone. People leave trails and anyone seeking a reference has long since learned to track people down as efficiently as does the homicide squad. You can try listing a peer who worked with you and knows your work as a reference. This works about 40 percent of the time if the organization you worked for is very large. There is a certain lethargy in many companies about checking references. If nothing about your conduct, application, or résumé looks suspicious, they may not check. Unfortunately, job hoppers almost always look suspicious.

Your best bet may be to submit copies of letters of reference from people with whom and for whom you worked. If the letters are glowing enough, present enough detail, and generally reek sincerity, you may lull the employer into accepting these in lieu of conducting his own check. You can rarely lull a personnel department unless the people are hopelessly faceless and overburdened to the degree that if you mess up, it won't come back to them.

Fifth, you have got to face unflinchingly the reactions you're going to get from people who've been burned by a job hopper who looked good, played it with sincerity, and moved on at an inopportune time. Like everyone else, job hoppers can have class. Those who do don't leave people in the lurch when they drift.

If you have no explanation, no context in which your job hopping makes sense, you'd best start working on one. There is simply no way to sell a new employer by acknowledging that you're a drifter who's looking for the ultimate high. The local drug pusher has higher standards for employees than that!

Sixth, don't get discouraged or desperate because you're not greeted with enthusiasm when you try to make the ultimate change, the one which you've promised yourself and anyone else who will listen is going to be right for you for at least three years. If your friends and colleagues from the trade associations seem leery of recommending you because they know you're a drifter, you'll have to sell them before they will sell anyone else on your behalf. Some of the people who helped you before may have taken a lot of flak when you drifted out in short order. Be prepared for their telling others that helping you is a high risk business. Accept this kind of feedback as realistic, possibly justified. The point is that, unless you can sell your friends on your newfound stability, you don't have a prayer of selling personnel professionals and the wary managers for whom they recruit.

Lots of reformed job hoppers turn to jelly at the prospect of the commitment they're expected to make when they finally have a choice. Can they stick it out? What if this job really isn't "it" either? Maybe there is no "it."

Internal or External

In the end, you have to decide whether your job-related problems are external or whether you need assistance from a therapist. If you do need help, you are prolonging your own pain by not getting it. It may be a question of straightening out your own priorities. You may be trying to become something you really have neither the talent nor the temperament to be. Job hopping reflects a frantic search for an environment that will support you. This often happens to people who want to manage people but lack the skills and personality to do so. The fact is that you can't put it off just because it's painful. The closer you move to forty, the harder it is to explain unstable behavior; even a society alleged to value "doing your own thing" expects more stable job patterns from people of a certain age.

Is it ever hopeless? As long as you're breathing, there's hope you'll fine someone willing to gamble on your stability and suitability against the odds of your track record. Keep in mind that no organization is truly permanent. People die; retire; leave; and change attitudes, positions, and power. Until there is some real permanence in organizations, your problem has a limited life.

Chapter 6
The Bad Reference

You resigned or were laid off. You begin immediately to look for a new job. You had lots of leads on positions you were entirely qualified to fill. Everybody in your considerable personal and professional network fed you rumors and genuine leads. Your experience, educational background, appearance, and personal style seemed fine. You got a raft of initial interviews. You furnished each prospect with all previous employers as references. You hadn't the slightest clue that this was a tactical error.

There had been no problems with your performance on your last job. Your written performance appraisals were fine, if not glowing. There was no hint of a problem. You had gotten regular raises. At no time did you realize that your performance was unsatisfactory—much less you'd get a bad reference. Even though you and the boss may not always have seen eye to eye, the parting was amiable. Certainly the boss never gave you a hint that your reference would be unfavorable.

'ROUND AND 'ROUND

You interview at a number of places: After the initial interview, which goes well, you wait a week or so, then call back to see what your status is. There is no explanaton as to why you haven't heard other than the standard refrain. "There are other candidates" or "We haven't made a decision." You get the unmistakable impression, however, that you are not going to get another interview. The person to whom you speak is barely polite, certainly not encouraging. You've been eliminated at the earliest stage.

Sometimes you may go through two or three interviews only, quite suddenly, to meet a dead end. Several people have gotten so far in the process as to have been offered jobs only to have the personnel office deny that an offer was made, in essence rescinding it. What went wrong?

SCUTTLED, YOU SAY!

It's likely that your former employer indicated, either explicitly or through innuendos, that you were unsatisfactory in some respect. The strongest negative would be if the boss indicated that the organization would not rehire you. There would be no need to go into performance appraisals or reasons. That one statement would be enough. As one personnel director said, "Anytime a boss says that the organization would not rehire a person he's off our list. We don't much care why."

It doesn't take much to discourage a prospective employer who has only met you once or twice. A chill in the former employer's voice, a hesitation, the pregnant pause, are quite enough. Why should the prospective boss check back one more job to see whether this is part of a pattern or just an isolated incident? Why confront you and ask for explanations? It's simpler just to drop you and look at other candidates. The greater the number of candidates for the job, the easier it is to drop one who might be a problem.

THE BAD NEWS

The job hunter is caught in a double bind. Suppose you know your boss dislikes you and will skunk your chances if possible. It's unthinkable to lie on the application. If you lie about your superior's name or skip the job entirely, there is always the possibility of someone finding out what you did after you're hired. Besides, most application forms demand a signed statement to the effect that "I certify that this material is true, complete, and correct to the best of my knowledge and belief. I understand if this information is misrepresented I can be dismissed for cause." That's pretty explicit.

On the other hand, if you do give all of the facts and a reference check is done, you won't get the job. If your boss sees this as a boss's ultimate weapon, you could spend months or even years looking for a job only to lose each one during the reference check. That's the nightmare many people conjure up. The facts are somewhat different.

THE GOOD NEWS

Luckily for job hunters only about 50 percent of all employers regularly and thoroughly check references. The system is by no means impenetrable. Checking is a lot of bother and may require several telephone calls to reach the right person. That person may stonewall and give nothing except a bare recital of facts. If the organizaton is in a different city, it's expensive to check long distance, especially if callbacks are needed.

Written reference checks aren't always answered promptly if at all. If a written request is sent and elicits no reply, you may be hired pending results. This is a break. You can be working at top speed making yourself liked and indispensable so that you'll be entrenched if the reference is not good.

A small organization may check but the person doing the checking is a bored clerk paid the minimum wage. That person's motivation to get full, correct information is much less than a prospective boss's would be. He or she may not try more than once or twice to reach the right person, or may simply pass it on as okay. Who will know? If you perform, the story has a happy ending and no one's any wiser.

How likely are you to have to face the reference problem during your working life? What can be done if your references are unfavorable? Statistically, service people, especially "knowledge" workers, whose performance appraisals are purely subjective—you're judged on your judgments—have about a one in five chance of meeting the problem. The stronger your convictions, opinions, and independence the more likely that you'll run up against someone who disagrees and means to make his or her opinion count.

If you work for a small business or a nonprofit group, your boss may be less restrained by legal considerations of defamation, libel, or ethics. He or she may give an uninhibited opinion out of ignorance. The boss may be so unaware of the law as to think he or she has carte blanche. Of such attitudes are the dreams of lawyers made! Large organizations have personnel departments that can screen reference calls and control the kinds of references given; they can threaten the careers of managers who don't toe the mark. Small ones frequently don't have any power to influence managers—much less enforce company policy.

MACHIAVELLI LIVES!

Ninety percent of all bad references stem from office politics, usually failure to get along with the boss or conflicts with coworkers or the organization's values. It's extremely rare for a person with serious skills deficiencies, petty theft problems, or other serious problems, to quit without finding another job first. At the least, he or she would try to find out what kind of reference can be expected. Individuals with severe problems recognize that there is a problem.

Ironically, employers are far less likely to report serious problems in reference checks because they fear legal action. They will, however, offer gratuitous comments on someone's personality, attitude, or work habits without a second thought, supposing that nobody can sue for this sort of thing. Apparently it never occurs to them that calling a person a "character" is just as harmful as calling him or her a thief. If someone doesn't get a job because of the reference, it hardly matters what was said. The end result is the same.

ALL ALONE IN ANOTHER TOWN

As a job hunter, the worst possible situation you can face is having left a job under a cloud and moved to another city. If you have few or no contacts in the new city, you are likely to have a lengthy job search. Companies that may be lax in checking references on local residences are often much more cautious with the newly arrived who have no local sponsors. If you are recommended by someone local, especially someone in the prospective employer's network, the clouds tend to clear. The path of least resistance, i.e., not checking, is, once again, probable.

Organizations, regardless of size or type, are most likely to check references carefully under the following circumstances.

1. You are changing careers and the shift is fairly radical. Former teachers who apply for jobs in business can expect a reference check, especially if they are leaving voluntarily and had tenure in the system. They will also be interviewed more exhaustively and by more people. Business people still think of teaching as an easy job, one which no one would leave voluntarily unless disaster loomed. "Why would someone give up a three-month paid vacation? There must be a problem."

2. An organization has a large personnel staff that views reference checks as an important, visible way to justify its existence. You may run into the underpaid clerk, but you may also run into someone trying to win his or her spurs by screening out the losers.

3. The organization's assets are portable. Banks, other financial institutions, and companies with many liquid assets will check regardless of the level of the job you've applied for or your remoteness from those assets. There's no need to knowingly invite a thief into the organization, and thieves are certainly aware of the opportunities in these organizations. The same is true with data processing operations involving credit cards. Computer theft is widespread and increasingly sophisticated.

4. Organizations with sensitive, innovative information are concerned with industrial spies. These organizations not only check formally through organizations but may also try to check informally. They may also want personal references and the names of former professors.

5. Organizations with access to secret or top secret information are concerned because they are government contractors. Before the organization can hire you in any sensitive area, you must get a security clearance; this includes a thorough reference and background check. This is a rigorous process; anything shaky in your background will come to light. You may or may not be given a chance to explain or amplify any negative information.

6. The interviewer smelled your fear when the subject of references came up. You didn't sound particularly fearful but your body language gave you away. Maybe you tried to gloss over questions about references. Somehow you aroused the interviewer's suspicions. There is certainly an element of human nature and curiosity involved. However, if you seem more than mildly concerned, you can be dropped from the process at this point, saving the organization the time and expense of a formal check.

7. You sold yourself inadequately to a risk avoider and the person can't decide what he or she thinks. The reference check is a device to allow your previous employer or employers to tip the decision one way or the other. It may be a copout because the prospect is trying to avoid making a decision. If you are up against a risk avoider, your prospects are not good. The prospective boss may actually expect your former boss to sell you. If your former boss is disinclined to do so, you're in trouble. Ditto if your former boss decides to unsell you.

8. Your background and experience are incongruent with your appearance or manner. You seem to have excellent credentials but personally you don't make a good impression. You may seem too young for as much experience as you say you have. You may look older than you really are. Somehow, without picking up the signals, you trampled a sacred cow. If the prospect expects all stable people to be married and you aren't, the reference check may be the boss's method of looking for confirmation of a particular assumption.

9. You did not come presold. The person you'd really be reporting to doesn't know you and so is going to rely more heavily on references to shore up or to sway his or her judgment. Nobody within the organization knows or can vouch for you. You are a victim of objective consideration. Unless your former boss puts on a very convincing show, you've probably lost the job.

10. The prospect has had a lot of turnover in the job and is heavily hedging all bets. Nobody is going to burn him or her again! If the interviewer picks up even a hint of job hopping during a reference check, you're in trouble. You don't really have to have changed jobs often. It's curtains if your boss suggests you were "restless."

11. You are over forty and were at your last job for ten or more years. The prospective employer—well aware of age discrimination—suspects you were fired. He or she wonders what you could have done. A check will be made.

MEET MY FRIEND JOE

It's axiomatic that if you come to the organization for the initial interview because someone recommended you or you were invited by the interviewer on the basis of a past relationship, the reference check is not nearly as important. Even a bad reference from your last boss may not deter someone from hiring you. The prospective boss may conclude that this was just an aberration. Better yet, you may be asked to explain what happened. A bad reference can be neutralized relatively easily if you get a chance to explain or to refute charges made by others. Fearing legal action and the loss of comradeship among employers, most prospective employers won't provide this opportunity unless they want you badly.

What can you do if you suspect that you have a reference problem? Do not panic and do not get into a shame or guilt mode. One of the terrors of the bad reference is that it feels like a character flaw. How can you tell your family and friends that you're getting a *bad* reference? They might secretly agree with the former boss's assessment. You feel very alone, helpless, and utterly victimized.

If you think rationally, you'll realize that nobody can keep you from getting a job permanently though they can delay your progress. You are not alone; you are not the first victim. You are one of a vast army to whom this has happened. Many people you know have been through it, but they've kept quiet about it. Don't perpetuate the conspiracy of silence with your intimates. Enlist their support. Your former colleagues may not realize that the boss is capable of this level of meanness, especially when they saw you as very competent. They need to know. It would be an act of mercy on your part to let them know. (Wait until you get a job before you warn them. It's a wonderful revenge.)

The numbers are with you; eventually you will find a manager too egotistical and too impatient to care about anybody else's judgment. If you sell him or her, that's enough. It may take many interviews, many disappointments, and many bleak periods before you run across such a jewel. Rather than wait for the Red Sea to part, here are some things you can do to diagnose and then neutralize the problem. You may even succeed in turning around the person who is speaking ill of you.

Did He Really Perform?

Find someone in a legitimate business who will call your former boss and ask for a reference. This person must be willing to go through all of the steps needed to assure your boss that he or she is serious about hiring you. You may want to rehearse the person to assure credibility. It's vital to have them ask key questions in sensitive areas. For instance, if you and the boss had a personality conflict, your surrogate must ask how you got along with people. The question that leads your boss to volunteer an opinion or make a statement is in order. That's what will happen during a real reference check. Without such a reading of the boss's reaction, you won't learn anything that will help you formulate a winning strategy.

This test is the only reliable way of finding out whether you have a reference problem. If you plan any legal action, it would be better to get a written reference. However, if you just want a reading on what's being said, an oral reference will suffice. Without finding out that you have a reference problem, you could be blowing interviews, be choosing the wrong kinds of job for which to apply, or be losing out for a variety of reasons. Often it's just a gut response to assume a bad reference because so many people aren't sure if they "read" the old boss correctly.

Once you know that your boss is giving you a bad reference, you have a number of alternatives, none of them risk free and none a sure thing. Still, they all beat playing the numbers game or "waiting it out." The more strapped you are financially the more you'll want to hurry the process.

Get the Letter First!

The best thing you could have done, and something you must do in the future, is to ask for a letter of reference before you leave the job. This pretests what you may be up against. If your boss refuses to give you a letter of recommendation, you will know, up front, that you have a serious obstacle to getting a new job. This will allow you to make plans and enlist some of the following techniques. It may also allow you to negotiate on the spot with the boss and see if anything can be done to ensure a good reference. If there's any doubt in your mind about the kind of reference you will get, find out before you leave. The boss can, and probably will, refuse to speak to you on the telephone once you find out you're being bad-mouthed. If he or she says favorable things in the letter and signs it, it will destroy him or her as a credible source if he or she retracts these statements orally at a later date.

Anyone can lie about what he or she will do. However, if you catch your boss off guard you may get a more honest reading.

Since you didn't or couldn't secure a letter before you left, there are other things you need to do now. Find a contact in each organization to which you are applying and ask that person to contact the person who will be your boss. Your contact can vouch for your competence and character. This may be less difficult to do than you might think. If you really search among friends and friends of friends before you apply, you'll turn up some helpers. This is by far the best, and in the long run, least costly method in terms of time and effort. It is also the best kind of reference you can get. If you are not active in your trade and professional associations, this is the strongest possible incentive to become so. That's the logical spot to find a pool of people from different organizations.

This is what you want to happen. You hear of a job at RBI Fantabulous Widgets, Inc. By careful research (that's seven telephone calls), you learn that one of your spouse's cousins works there. Depending on the nature of the relationship, you call him or your spouse does. Explain that you're thinking of applying and ask what he thinks. If you explain how much you think you'd be interested in the job and ask for his advice, he may just offer to tell the potential interviewer that he knows you and can vouch for you. There are risks, especially if you don't do well at the job and your contact is called to task. You will have to assess how much risk you and your contact will assume. Contacts are usually willing to do this unless asked by the potential interviewer for a money-back guarantee.

Mercy, Please!

If you have no other option, you may find it strategic to level with the interviewer from the personnel department and throw yourself on his or her mercy. If you've done a good job of selling yourself, you'll have a chance. This doesn't always work. Most personnel people would as soon be drawn and quartered as take a risk. In leveling with personnel, you're asking someone to take a risk. The less secure personnel as a department is within the organization, the less likely the person is to do this.

On the other hand, if the interviewer has a quota to fill, an impossible time frame, and demanding managers screaming for human sacrifice, you may get some help. As one interviewer said, "If a candidate sells me, I'm much more likely to try selling him or her to a potential boss. Despite the popular perception that I'm here to keep people out of the organization unless they're perfect!"

Throw yourself on the mercy of the person you'd be working for and explain, with as few accusations and value judgments as you can, what happened and why you left or were fired. Do this only if you are certain a reference check will eliminate you as a serious candidate. If you have chosen a prospective boss with any care, you may find that he or she has met this problem in the past and isn't much spooked by one bad reference. If the prospective boss is spooked and can't understand how such a thing could happen unless you really were incompetent, look elsewhere.

Among the bosses of the world are a fairly large number who've traveled the same road themselves; out of every five bosses, as many as two may have experienced similar situations. Or perhaps one in ten is the rule in your particular job field.

Call the personnel manager at your former company and explain what is going on. If the personnel manager thinks that your boss is going to cause the organization a problem, even if it's only bad publicity, someone is likely to go to your boss's boss and put the heat on.

Depending on your state's unemployment compensation structure, your former employer's personnel department may have another incentive to help you. If keeping you off somebody else's payroll is going to cost your former employer money, that's a powerful incentive to intervene. One of the personnel department's jobs is to monitor and control unemployment insurance costs.

Personnel can't keep you from getting fired even if you are right and the boss wrong. But, most personnel people can and will intervene if there's even the hint of a lawsuit or added unemployment compensation expense. Make your intentions clear. You are better off if you call yourself rather than having a lawyer call. Personnel may think the situation is still salvageable if they hear from you. If they hear from your lawyer, they may not exert themselves to the same degree. They may also run to corporate counsel and then you'll have to get involved with them. Limit the conflagration whenever you can.

Be prepared for personnel to be completely unaware of your boss's position. It may take some time for anyone in the department to get together both the facts and the courage to pressure your boss.

Call your former boss and explain that you know he or she is giving you a bad reference. Don't write a letter unless you are prepared to have a lawyer, experienced in defamation and libel law, look it over before you mail it. If your boss stonewalls or admits that he or she is giving you a bad reference, you may want to suggest that you have engaged a lawyer. This may not move the person; on the other hand, it may. Most people will go to some lengths to avoid confrontations involving lawyers, even if they don't have to bear the expense personally. Remember, your boss has to protect his or her career first. Any manager who gets involved in a lawsuit is unlikely to emerge unsullied; companies hate lawsuits, regardless of who's right.

Threatening your former boss is a last resort. There are so many ways he or she can put you off, deny your charges, or simply get angry and tell you off. It may cause the boss to go out of his or her way to hurt your career, even at great risk to his or her own. Until now the boss has just given you a poor reference. Once enraged, he or she may actively try to hurt you by making telephone calls to colleagues, telling your former colleagues what a troublemaker you are, etc.

Meet My Lawyer, Larry Lawsuit

If it's any comfort, you do have legal rights. People have gone to court and won damages from employers who defamed them to prospective employers. Justice is very slow, however, and the settlement you win may come as long a three, four, or five years after litigation begins. There can be costly appeals and delays. Winning a court settlement, or even an out-of-court settlement, may not make up for the years of anxiety and unemployment. It's not an option to consider lightly.

But if all else fails, get a lawyer and have him or her begin with judicious pressure. The lawyer who handled the closing on your condominium is not the person you should hire. Only a very streetwise defamation lawyer with superb negotiating skills can help you. A lawsuit is the last thing you want. You need someone who can frighten people, not just sue them. A lawsuit could hurt your career more than a bad reference and for a much longer period of time. Legal action is absolutely the last resort. Never go to court until every other option has been tried and exhausted, or until you have beaten the numbers game and gotten a job.

Your best strategy is to get a job through your contacts, rendering references unnecessary. That's why making and keeping business contacts is so critical to your success. Once you get a new job, go to court and cause your former employer as much trouble as you like, but only after you're firmly entrenched somewhere else.

If you were fired from a job, you can use the same steps to secure references. Being fired is such a trauma that people often spill their guts to prospective employers without any idea that they may be getting a decent reference anyway. If you are fired, always test the water by asking for a written letter. If there's a serious problem, begin immediately to plan ways around it.

Chapter 7

Reverse Discrimination

Among women's organizations reverse discrimination is "The Problem That Has No Name." It's simply not talked about except as a threat. With men, it is different. Men between twenty-two and thirty-five are facing a whole new set of potential knockouts in their careers. The women's movement has forsaken confrontation for intensified, all-out competition. Many men are only vaguely aware of what's happened and what's coming. This strategy of all-out competition can't help but affect the men with whom women are competing, especially the men who think that no heat means no fire. If the women aren't marching, these men reason, they must have withdrawn. Not so.

BREAD, NOT CRUMBS

Women make up almost 50 percent of current MBA candidates, 50 percent of undergraduate accounting majors, some 45 percent of law students, and almost 40 percent of medical and dental students. They are not pursuing these demanding programs so that they can abandon them for babies and soap operas in a few years.

Nursing schools and dental hygienist programs, for instance, are certainly aware of the change in women's aspirations. The rallying cry they hear is, "Why be a nurse when you can be a doctor? Why be a dental hygienist when you can be a dentist?" By extension, why be a paralegal when you can be a lawyer; a bookkeeper when you can be a CPA? Why settle for crumbs when you could have the whole loaf? It doesn't take even the least assertive of females long to see the bottom line difference on a salary chart. This is especially true if she gets a little insight from her Uncle Sam and the national and local media.

Women have learned something very important from the sixties and the seventies: do what you want but don't alert the enemy to your strategy by talking about your intentions publicly. They also learned that all-out competition is not only important, but mandatory. Many have decided that this particular game is more than worth the ante. As a result, recognizing the relative contempt and bad press—not to mention male paranoia—generated by the radical feminists and the organized opposition, the eighties woman will not only play the game by the rules, she will fool all but the most perceptive observer. Less observant types won't even realize that there is a serious revolution in process.

The new woman will abandon radicalism. She'll look, act, and compete in ways no man could fault. Her manners and demeanor would please Emily Post. She also will have a competitive advantage because sometimes, in some places, the long arm of fear of the Equal Employment Opportunity Commission (EEOC) will help her, though she would be foolish to count on it. She rarely does. She's counting on herself and others like her.

The new woman also has the competitive advantage of having been toughened by a lack of family support—sometimes open opposition, a lack of social support, and the need to keep her eye on securing her place. She is a total realist. Any surprises she has will be pleasant ones because she expects the worst. She has no illusions. She doesn't count on luck or good intentions to help her.

THE DRAGON LADY

This woman controls her own fertility, submerges her emotions, and aims for the top. While her older sisters wrestle endlessly with guilt over the "balanced lifestyle," i.e., balancing husband, children, career, and all of the angst of role conflicts, the eighties woman thinks in terms of her ambitions. She doesn't see sacrifices but opportunities; she is a woman of whom John Calvin and his ilk would heartily approve.

That's a profile of the women who will get MBA's and other advanced degrees in the 1980s. There will always be throwbacks to the Kinder, Küche, Kirche group who are simply hedging their bets by getting degrees while husband hunting among the most success-prone group. The majority, however, despite their soft, smiling, man-pleasing exteriors, have more in common with China's Dowager Empress Tz'u-hsi, known by her contemporaries as the "Dragon Lady," than with future converts to Phyllis Schlafly's cause.

TOTAL WAR, NOT *TOTAL WOMAN*

Thus a great many men face the unthinkable in the 1980s: serious, well-prepared competitors willing to pay the price as well as reverse discrimination. It's a potential career knockout. Look at the facts. If you are male, no manager with the I.Q. and savvy of a retarded sheep is going to "take you into his confidence" and explain the facts of life. He can't tell you that the organization has to play catch-up with its female and minority employees and that it's going to do so at your expense. At best, you might leave. At the worst, you may decide you are going to win a victory for men; unlike Brian Weber, who lost his reverse discrimination suit, you are going to turn affirmative action around with your case.

If no one tells you that your career has stalled because the organization has to advance women and minorities more quickly, you may stay. You will continue to produce at the same high level you always have. Top management's desperate, if chauvinistic hope, is that an opening will appear for you before you catch on to the game. You may also lose some races because, objectively, you're not the best-qualified candidate, and just being male isn't worth what it used to be. You may find this shocking, outrageous, and depressing all at once.

WATCHING THE SIGNALS

There are many signals that indicate whether or not your career is going to run aground on organizational affirmative action necessities. Be aware of what they are and be prepared to act in your own interest.

1. **Every internal opening is announced to generate the greatest number of minority applicants.** In the past, this was a sham covering some manager's attempt to legitimize promoting a favorite son—rarely a favorite daughter or minority. Job posting was a formality and a corporate fantasy. With more sophisticated number crunching and a cutting edge to competition on the part of women and minorities, that ratification process is being challenged and in some cases defeated. At the least, it frightens those

who were using the system. At the most, there's now genuine competition. Even if your manager tried to sneak you in, his or her action may not go unchallenged. Personnel is watching and, in this area anyway, its collective opinion counts.

2. The organization has been cited for affirmative action violations or thinks it might be. It's much harder for men in the organization to advance if top management is biting its collective nails at the thought of an EEOC suit. The thought of a suit is worse than being in the throes of a suit. Most organizations will go to almost any length to avoid actual litigation. They may begin by rapidly promoting all competent, and a few clearly incompetent but available, females as a way to stave off hostile government action. Once under siege, with lawyers at the ready, management tends to return to its old patterns because the worst has already happened. It's a cleanup operation at that point. Top management always hopes that the government-imposed settlement will be less far-reaching than what the corporation itself might have done in a moment of panic.

3. Some of the women in the organization have legitimate grievances. If and when these women are satisfied, they will still have infected other women with a bone-deep, richly justified distrust of management and a desire to examine their own careers and prospects. This is sometimes called "consciousness raising" and you don't have to organize and hold meetings to do it. If one secretary escapes her typewriter and coffee-making duties, ten others congratulate her in the very same breath that they use to press management for more of the same. This ferment will spill over into the personnel department.

Personnel will shudder collectively as it becomes even more cautious and urges top management to do the same. Every man up for promotion will be examined more carefully because "the women are watching." (Do you remember Alfred Hitchcock's movie *The Birds?* In companies under siege you often get the feeling that top management sees itself in the telephone booth with the birds sky-diving at the glass.) The women who are watching and waiting for change have no power except the implied power to cause trouble and to foster the rearrangement of what management had always thought were agreeable relationships.

4. **The industry's track record of promoting women is miserable.** For instance, among the "Big Eight" public accounting firms, the number of women with degrees in accounting, certified and licensed, and with years of suitable experience is not reflected in the number of women partners. One of the largest firms has more than a thousand male partners and two female partners. Another had no women partners at all even though they have many women managers; managers are one level below partners. The general sense of impending doom in those firms is

palpable; the feeling is that the minute the government finishes with banks, it will move to public accounting. The EEOC is unlikely to start its campaign with the fiftieth-largest firm when the "Big Eight" or "Big Sixteen" are so obviously in need of "help."

As a male, your prospects for partnership are dimming as all of those fresh, bright women decide that partnership is the ticket. It will be startling how quickly suitable women come out of the woodwork and are turned into partners when the government turns the screws. The federal government and many local government units are important audit and consulting clients. This change in women's prospects for partnerships will only confirm what every woman senior (two levels down) and manager has always known. There has not been a lack of competent women but a lack of top management's recognition of competent women. The problem has been compounded in accounting because the process of voting for partners has seemed to be an obstacle. How can men be forced to vote for women? The EEOC will help these partners see how easy it is to vote for women when not voting for them affects profits and profit sharing. Half a loaf is *always* better.

5. Top management has drawn its wagons into a circle because it is constitutionally unwilling or unable to promote women. Management hopes to generate enough support for a suicidal gesture, the "I'd rather be right" syndrome. The fallout won't help your career because the trouble with affirmative action won't go away. The energy needed to fight a long and bitter war against change is often the very energy that is needed to keep the organization on track and profitable.

The case of Alan Bakke, who sued the University of California at Davis because he was denied admission to medical school as a white person, was seen as a reverse discrimination victory. Although the U.S. Supreme Court, in its 1978 decision, ruled that Bakke should be admitted to medical school, it supported the idea that race could be considered in selecting students.

Brian Weber sued Kaiser Aluminum and Chemical Corporation because he thought he'd been illegally kept out of a skilled-job training program because he was white. Fifty percent of the training slots had been reserved for minority people. In 1979, the U.S. Supreme Court decided to solidly support affirmative action programs. The court ruled that employers could give special consideration to minority groups in selecting participants for job-training programs. Both cases were race discrimination cases, but women, as well as minority people, are reaping the benefits of the decisions.

That doesn't mean that reverse discrimination suits are dead. Despite the EEOC's brave talk, there is likely to be a case narrow enough, blatant enough, with a lawyer clever enough, to win a limited victory in the near future. How does this help your situation? It doesn't. You are unlikely to benefit from any such suits unless there is a dramatic and wholly unexpected reversal in the entire civil rights movement. That's possible only if the government drops its efforts at vigorous enforcement. The poor little match girl now wields a very large stick. Since the protected classes, primarily women and minorities, are also large blocs of voters, only members of Congress with strong suicidal tendencies are going to recommend cutbacks.

Knowing this, what should and can you do to help yourself advance at the rate you'd prefer in the face of unrelenting and formidable competition?

NO HELP, NO SYMPATHY

Your organization, frightened by negative publicity and the rising cost of defending litigation, cannot be publicly helpful or even sympathetic to your problems. Whatever steps you take to protect and advance your career will have to be taken alone. You may want to give thought to some of the following strategies.

1. The federal government can't get around to everybody. Difficult as this may be to believe when you look at the size of the federal bureaucracy, it's true. Some industries are easier targets than others because they have more females and obvious traditions of nonadvancement of even the most overqualified women. Stay away from these industries. Accounting and banking come to mind. They are, and are likely to remain, under intense government scrutiny for years to come. Industries with highly technical jobs, particularly heavy-equipment manufacturing firms, would be better bets even if you are in marketing or another nontechnical area. There are fewer women competing for the job you want in these areas. Many women just don't think about jobs in these industries. It will be easier to convince management you are the best-qualified candidate—the only one likely to fit in and succeed. Look at small companies. The government prefers to do its shopping at the giant chains and not "mom and pop" enterprises. This is a deliberate strategy; there is more publicity, larger settlements, and hopefully more fire to frighten other recalcitrant corporate executives into getting busy developing their own affirmative action plans.

Management skills are important to a wide variety of industries and to companies within those industries. You have a great range of choices. Stay away from regulated industries such as communications and utilities. Ma Bell (American Telephone and Telegraph) and some of her daughters have already been hit as have a number of utilities companies. Don't select a company with a large government contract. Every government contract has a compliance provision. That compliance may be achieved at your expense. There are plenty of backward pockets in a variety of industries filled with profitable companies. It's your job to find them.

Remember that the companies you read about as having discrimination problems are only a smattering of the companies that could employ you.

2. If you must work for a company with affirmative action programs in ferment, look for the ones that have promoted women above their levels of competence. Companies engaged in aggressive tokenism are good candidates. If you can arrange to follow close behind a woman who is in over her head, your chances of getting a crack at her job when she washes out are fairly good. This is also true of racial minorities who have failed. You get the backlash vote. This may seem cold-blooded. Remember, if you don't protect your interests, nobody else is even remotely likely to do so. You don't have an advocate because you are not supposed to need one.

3. Support the Equal Rights Amendment and universal conscription. Your best hope is that both will be passed. Then, with reinstatement of government registration and conscription, née the draft, women won't be able to gain a substantial competitive advantage while you're off toting a gun. They'll be in the same boat. If only men are drafted, your competitors will be finishing their educational programs, advanced degrees, and internships and scooping up all the best jobs while you're doing time in the armed forces.

You can't count on an individual manager who's trying to fill a job to hold it for a man off playing

Lawrence of Arabia. Despite government propaganda, an MBA graduate isn't going to learn much that's useful or make many useful contacts in the trenches or in some wretched outpost here or abroad. The armed forces are no match for the experience (and money) you'd get at General Motors or FMC Corporation. Being out of the mainstream also presents the chilling prospect of putting you permanently a step behind; catching up is impossible. The Dragon Ladies can move very far, very fast when they have the field to themselves.

Most women retired to the kitchen when the "boys" came home after World War II. Never again—today's women will see your enforced withdrawal from the scene as a golden opportunity. They think that the women who retreated in 1945 were the ultimate example of what not to do. (So do some of the women who did it in 1945; they are trumpeting this interpretation to their daughters and granddaughters.)

4. Use the old boy network. After all, it has to be valuable, otherwise penetrating it and plugging it wouldn't be such an obsession with upwardly mobile women everywhere. The network is highly developed in many industries. Locate the companies that reward good old boys and join up. These will tend to be smaller companies headed by an owner-manager who either does not know about the EEOC or knows and doesn't care. The owner may be hedging his bets as to when the feds will get around to him. His bet may be never, as long as he goes through the motions of looking for qualified women.

5. Don't air your grievances. Complaints and shouts of "it's not fair" haven't proved to be solid competitive advantages for women, have they? There are women smarter, more creative, more political, and more competitive than you are. They are willing to submerge every other aspect of their lives to rise on the job. Don't underestimate them—it could be fatal to your prospects. Complaining about this state of affairs is useless. If anyone gets discouraged and goes away, it will be you. These women can positively smell victory; you couldn't get rid of them under any circumstances. Complaining about what you're up against sounds as if you're worried about the competition. This is not an attractive position nor does it inspire male management above you to have confidence in your abilities. If you falter, you may convince the most chauvinistic among your superiors that perhaps he's misjudged your female competitors.

6. Expect to work harder and longer to secure the opportunities your father would have considered his birthright. The 1980s are not going to be boom times. The economic opportunity pie may be larger, even after adjustment for inflation, but anytime more people compete for a slice, there are bound to be some people whose slice will be smaller. Between inflation and the economic downturn, you can practically see your particular slice shrinking.

7. Expect to move from job to job internally, and from organization to organization. Organizational gypsying is going to be a career style in the 1980s. You won't find one safe berth to ride out the storm unless you own the company. And éven that's not a sure bet; if the EEOC runs out of big targets, it may sink its teeth into the little guys. In a revolution, no one is immune.

8. You may reach détente with a particular woman at a particular time. (There is nothing like a working wife to give a man a different perspective—not to mention cash.) Unless you are prepared to organize your brothers into a reverse *Lysistrata* and withhold sex until women leave corporate life altogether, détente may be your best option. Even if you tried withholding, there are always strike breakers to reckon with.

If détente is your aim, don't look for companionship within your own organization. It's uncomfortable to cuddle a direct competitor—acknowledged or not. Samson and Delilah come to mind. If you are looking for a supportive, rather than competitive, relationship, look for someone who is not now, nor likely to be, directly competing with you for a job. Nor should you make overtures to people who strike you as your clones. It's all too close for domestic harmony.

As one man who dated a systems analyst from a rival corporation reported, "Don't ever date someone who's in the same field. A close relationship can't develop if every time you talk about business you can't help but worry that she knows more, is getting ahead, or plans to use the information against you somehow. It's too much pressure."

9. Clean up your act and avoid making implacable enemies. You should never, not even in jest, ask a a married working woman, regardless of relative organizational rank, what her husband thinks about her career unless you are prepared to duck or you know that the person you are questioning is *the* Phyllis Schlaffy or *the* Marabel Morgan (author of *The Total Woman*). Women, whether the one who puts fresh paper towels in the washrooms or the one who is director of corporate public relations, consider this question a deadly, deliberate insult. What does your wife, sweetheart, or roommate think about your career? Even a man in his eighties (who may remember an earlier generation of women's liberationists and is, therefore, unlikely to ask the question) can't get away with this.

Single women feel exactly the same antipathy when asked what their parents think about their careers. The implication in both cases is that moment must *belong* to someone and that title to the property is held by parents until passed to a husband.

The object of your question, particularly if she's a Dragon Lady, won't respond rudely. She may smile and either answer or fob off your question. She will remember and wait until she can get even, which according to her viewpoint she has every incentive to do. She'll also blacken your name in every new girl network to which she belongs. Who needs that?

10. Keep your sense of humor and try not to drown while stomping your own sour grapes. Losing your perspective won't help and may be a career knockout in itself. Bitching depresses everybody. Top management is still watching. They need you to help keep up male spirits and macho generally, and despite greater competition, there are still plenty of opportunities. All women aren't lined up with Tz'u-hsi—just a few very visible ones who may be in your way temporarily. Your most important competitor may still chuck it all to raise children, though it's best not to count on this. She might be willing, but her husband, the first liberated man, may be counting on her income to keep them both in Nikons and Porsches.

11. Don't buy any management promises and don't take any advice from men in their sixties with non-working wives and married pregnant daughters. Their ideas on female competitiveness are entirely theoretical and right out of the Dark Ages. They haven't a clue as to what you face. The women in their lives are into pots and pans, not plots and plans. With the best will in the world, they underestimate the potential knockout of Dragon Ladies with Uncle Sam as enforcer.

12. Maintain as much flexibility in your attitudes and career plans as you can. Statistically, most people change careers several times between entry into the work force and retirement. If one industry gets too crowded or is under too much attack to be comfortable, be prepared to move on and to apply your skills to another kind of business. Remember that industries with labor shortages have more opportunities for everybody. Some industries will boom in the 1980s. Keep up with what's going on in your industry and you'll be able to spot trends and act appropriately. Don't wait until the last light goes out before you move.

13. Don't take the attack on your supposed rights and historic privileges personally. Minorities and women aren't out to get you *personally* because they don't *know* you personally. They are not competing with you as a human being or as a worker; they are competing for the money and status they think you have and they want.

If it's any comfort, your position—having to pay for the mistakes of past generations of men and businesses—does excite a certain sympathy from some of the most ardent feminists. They empathize with you even if they do so secretly. Many also feel that they are being made to pay for someone else's rule changes. They, like you, weren't consulted and didn't get to vote.

For pure fellow feeling and commiseration, try the women, mostly in their forties and fifties, who, after twenty plus years of playing tennis, decorating houses, raising children, entertaining, cooking well, and looking great, were abruptly fired because George decided that the only meaningful relationship possible was with Sally Career. Sally Career did none of the foregoing. She worked and competed with you! Like you, these older women worked under a set of now discredited assumptions. They are every bit as frustrated, bruised, and unhappy as you are. Misery loves company! Maybe you and they can provide mutual support and comfort until they decide that competition is all and join the Dragon Ladies.

14. Male camaraderie will be affected when minority males move ahead of you. The war between the sexes now becomes the war between the haves and the have nots. This will disturb such male bonding as may have existed.

In the end, graceful accommodation, with every effort to protect your own career while acknowledging at least some of the legitimate claims of your competitors, will do more for your career than would either passive or active resistance. In fact, you might mount a deliberate strategy of cooperation that could lull your competitors into false sense of having achieved a major victory. With just such strategies are wars won and sanities saved!

Chapter 8

The Fallen Warrior and the Public Failure

Public debacles obsess us all—the assembly-line worker's call-down before peers as much as Richard Nixon's career crisis (loss of the presidency and public digrace). Many people so dread any kind of public or even private embarrassment that they become confirmed risk avoiders. Why strive when it's so much more comfortable to be less conspicuous, if also less successful?

It might take some of the sting out of public failure and provide some comfort to realize you can recover and even move up a bit by fighting back. The grace under pressure that Ernest Hemingway so admired has professional as well as personal value. Whether it's a lost promotion trumpeted throughout the organization or being tagged with a failed project, you can recover and move ahead if you know what you're doing.

THE FALLEN WARRIOR

You and a peer were neck and neck for a major promotion. Your colleagues, family, and friends assumed you were the front runner. They were pricing champagne for the victory celebration. Your boss called you in and told you that Jackie had gotten the promotion, and that you were runner-up. The public announcement was made and there was a dignified silence from everyone on your behalf. Your office supporters told you privately that Jackie was not half as qualified, and that you should have been the one. Even the grapevine registered measurable convulsions of surprise.

Worse for you than losing the promotion you wanted is being publicly branded a loser because you were passed over. You may have been unaware of the competition. You didn't know what might have been until it was already a fact. Even if you had no particular interest in the job, not having been offered it may rankle. This is especially true if everyone assumed you were dying for the job. They may even convince you that you were or should have been interested.

Perhaps you have been left out of plans for a major redistribution of power, mayhap demoted during a reorganization. It will still feel and look as if there had been a contest that you lost.

What now? This scenario, not uncommon in the seventies, will be increasingly common in the eighties, especially among baby boom people. More people competing for fewer openings will create more losers. If something like this happens to you, it can seem to be a real career knockout. The problem is going through a public failure puts you in the worst possible position to analyze what happened and to develop a strategy to advance your career, not just salvage it.

If promotions were made according to merit, life would be simpler—especially if merit were measurable. But they aren't and it isn't. So you're left in the realm of trying to guess, with very little real knowledge to support your guess, about what may have spoiled the deal.

OUT OF THE GATE

Let's look at the way most such situations develop. Anytime there's competition between two apparently equally qualified individuals, there must be a loser. That loser will be branded so publicly because it's impossible to have two or more people actively competing in private. When management sets up a horse race, everybody in the internal office network can be expected to pick a favorite. The closer the competition, the more speculation there will be. In some offices, employees form pools and bet on the outcome if the competition is heated enough. Management might not understand that it's encouraging the winner/loser syndrome, nevertheless it's a fact.

Everybody would like to win publicly and lose privately. This has never been possible and never will be. A great many organizations, through job posting, advancement interviews, and the process of ratification used to promote people, have made the losers as prominent as the winners. The process even tends to co-opt competitors who might not have wanted to compete. In other words, management has raised the ante for competition. The results of higher stakes are greater losses for some. If the company is concerned about affirmative action, this is especially likely to happen. As the personnel director of one *Fortune* 500 company said, "We wouldn't dare promote anyone here without interviewing and considering any and all possible candidates. Another method buys unlimited trouble."

If you lose one of these races you suffer an initial shock through which you have to live before you can get on with your job and your career. Once you've recovered, it's appropriate to do some analyzing. What went wrong? How can you deal with your feelings so that your career won't suffer?

If you were a front runner who lost out, you are going to feel depressed, angry, and wronged, all at the same time. The more you had counted on the promotion, the stronger these emotions will be. The way you deal with your feelings, not the fact that you didn't get the promotion, will be the key to what happens next in your career. In order to treat this as a temporary setback rather than a career knockout, you have to analyze what went wrong and what your next step should be.

Ph.D. or Master's?

A chemical company had two apparently equally qualified candidates vying for the position of production supervisor in a key plant. One had a Ph.D., one a master's degree. The Ph.D. had less experience and more theoretical knowledge, the master's person the reverse. For eighteen months, management wavered in deciding who would get the job. As the months went by, it was obvious that whoever lost would have to leave just to save face. The great delay in making the decision was a result of top management's desperate search for a compromise. The individual with the master's degree eventually won. Even though a new position of comparable importance was created for the Ph.D., he left after three months to become associate professor of chemical engineering at a university. Before leaving, he aired all of his feelings—his sense of outrage, feeling of loss, and desire to ensure his rival's failure. Even after he removed himself from the scene, both management and the winner had trouble rallying other employees to get on with the work. The contest had occupied everyone in the plant for months to the exclusion of every other problem and speculation.

Revenge: Not So Sweet

Revenge has been a classic pattern among the vanquished; leave and do as much as possible before leaving to get even with the management and the winner. The problem is that revenge is a high-risk game. Nobody in top management is likely to forget the Ph.D.'s lack of professionalism. Should the academic world fail him, he may find his references from the chemical company far from glowing. The story of his behavior is likely to be trotted out and retold in loving detail every time a similar situation arises.

Of course, management behaved stupidly in letting the contest go on for eighteen months. Making the decision cleanly and quickly within days or weeks of the announcement of the opening would have caused far less of a flap. You don't have to be a social scientist to predict that, once a contest is announced or the contestants know that there is a contest, speculation will intensify as time passes. Management people, however, often seem determined to act in their own, and the organization's, worst interests.

If you are faced with a similar situation, find out whether you were turned down in favor of a more qualified candidate (however that may be defined) or if the turndown is part of a pattern before you decide whether or not to go. If you can find out why, it would be helpful, especially if there were no significant differences between you and the successful candidate. It's important to find out whether or not you have been secretly branded as unpromotable.

I Want to Know . . .

How much information can you expect from your boss? To a large extent this will depend on the use the boss expects you to make of this information. Many managers will give employees a fairly straightforward appraisal of the facts in the selection process if they think the information will anchor them to the organization and clear the air. The problem arises in really close races; the closer the race, the less rational the reasons may sound to the losers. If management can't point out a clear qualitative difference, if, in fact, the selection was political, or, worse yet, the loser was much more qualified in almost everybody's eyes, the manager will probably try to be evasive.

If you were the loser, it won't be enough just to know that the decision was political. You need to know why you were less politically desirable than the winner. Studying your rival may supply this information. Getting a reading on your boss's perceptions of the two of you would be more helpful. In any case, you ought to start with a detailed analysis of your strengths and weaknesses—personal and political—compared to your rival's. In the future, you will want to do this before any decision is made, not after. No matter how overwhelming your strengths seem as opposed to those of your rival, catalogue both strengths and weaknesses. You must be as objective as possible.

If your boss won't talk specifically about how the decision was made, you may be tempted to ask peers for their analysis. This is a mistake. They will want to protect themselves politically. If you seem to be gathering information, people are going to ascribe all sorts of motives to your information gathering, none of which may be correct. The speculation can only hurt you.

Outside Help Helps

Although you are working in an internal vacuum in many respects, there is a source of help outside the company that you can tap with less risk. Get together with someone who knows your organization, either a former employee from your department or a person in a similar job in a competitor's shop. Explain the facts in confidence. Ask for that person's analysis. You may learn a great deal. If you find out that your rival is the latest in a line of similarly endowed candidates to be promoted, you may change your mind abut how good your chances were to begin with. Keep in mind that people working for promotion aren't going to be motivated if they learn that most of them are not really in the running. Unless you get this kind of information, you'll never know where you stand.

Your boss may assume that by keeping you dangling he or she will get a better performance from you at less cost to the organization. This is a commonly held philosophy. It may seem cold-blooded, but it's definitely in the organization's best interests. If all the people destined to be "also-rans" knew what was in store for them, there would be no Indians for the chiefs.

The longer management strings out the promotion process, the more anxious they are to keep all candidates working at top speed. Delays in announcing the decision serve the same purpose. Once it's known who the winner will be, the loser may either slack off or leave.

TWEEDLEDEE, TWEEDLEDUM

Assuming that you and your rival were very much alike in terms of experience, education, and length of service with the organization, why did you lose?

Perhaps your rival appeared to be more committed to the organization. Management may have judged you as ready to bolt if a better opportunity were offered elsewhere. Whether or not this assumption is true is immaterial if someone acted on it.

Your rival may have had a sponsor higher up in the company of whom you were unaware. It wasn't the open race you thought it was.

Your boss may personally prefer the company of your rival. The two of them may have more in common personally or professionally than the two of you.

Your boss may have seen you as a potential threat to his or her job and decided your rival was less a threat.

You're being saved for something bigger down the road and nobody has thought to mention this to you. The larger the organization, the more likely this is to happen. Management may have a consolation position in mind if you bear up well under this disappointment.

You failed at some fairly insignificant task but your boss judged you as likely to fail again. You may not be aware of this or you may have underestimated the importance of the failure. You may have refused to do something as a matter of principle. Unfortunately, the principle upon which you made your stand was not seen as a matter of principle by your boss.

You have been too active politically within the organization outside your own area. People assume that you're neither trustworthy nor loyal. Your personal loyalty to your boss has been questioned. Never underestimate this as a cause of problems. A boss trying to build a fiefdom resents vassals who can't be counted on.

You seem too independent, not enough of a team player. Independent people cause waves and disturb the tranquility of the work group. You can't be bought and therefore you may not go along with your boss at a critical juncture. Bosses hate surprises more than anything.

Your rival was needier. You have a working spouse or parents with money. This is a favorite, if unpublicized, rationale of nonprofit groups, who often see themselves as agents for redistribution of income.

The list of causes is open-ended. Only you can decide which, if any, fit your situation. There is an explanation. It's worth trying to ferret out if only because you need some credible explanation in order to put your own anger and depression to rest. You are unlikely to get rid of those negative feelings without finding an explanation. As one woman who had twice been passed over for a supervisory position said, "I wouldn't mind losing if I knew why. It's nerve-racking not to know what went wrong. Even changing jobs might not help if it meant I would face the same problem somewhere else."

Once you've determined a probable cause, ask yourself if anything can be done to prevent a repetition. If your boss is not your strong supporter, and if he or she is firmly entrenched, you don't have a prayer. Begin thinking in terms of a transfer or a move out of the organization. This is particularly true for women up against a boss's preconceptions of the role of women. If he's convinced that women are a temporary force in the job market, you had best consider alternatives. Even the government can't ensure equitable treatment in one specific situation with one specific boss. Pack it in and move on.

Moving Out Carefully

Once you've decided to move on, you'll need a strategy to prevent a repetition of your loss. You will want to be extremely careful in job hunting. This may take time so cover yourself at your present job even as you look elsewhere. Remember that if you make your boss or anybody else too uncomfortable, a way can be, and will be, found to get rid of you.

If you're going to be at all comfortable at your present job, buying yourself thinking time in which to ensure that your next job will be more productive, you will have to do two things. One, you must congratulate your rival and wish him or her well as sincerely as if you weren't the loser. This will defuse a lot of the electricity and excitement generated by the contest. It will demonstrate that you are a person with working class and a team player. It will stop much of the gossip and speculation about what you will do now. Men who lost to women and don't do this are especially vulnerable to criticism. The woman will feel it keenly and remember it forever. Don't aggravate the problem by turning it into an equal rights standoff.

Second, you must continue to produce at the same high level you did when you were a serious candidate. If your performance slacks off even slightly, the word will be out in a flash. This will brand you as a loser in a way that actually losing the promotion did not. Do not underestimate how patiently many people are awaiting this very outcome. People who supported the winner are aching for you to slack off so that they can point out, once and for all, how superior the winner really is. You will rob them of a lot of satisfaction if you redouble your efforts. This kind of revenge is marvelous.

Do not talk about your feelings with anyone even remotely connected with work. Give no one your honest opinion unless you are prepared to see it, word for word, on the wall of the lunchroom. Confide in one peer, one employee in a distant department, and you might as well send around a memo. If asked how you feel, be noncommittal. Say, "Well it always hurts to lose but it happens to everyone occasionally." Don't get sucked into comparing yourself and the winner or into analyzing the outcome. That kind of situation only offers a temptation to say something you'll regret.

Unless you can resist the temptation to air your feelings through the informal network, think seriously about leaving. Transmitting your feelings through the grapevine will keep the atmosphere charged and lengthen the time it takes for people to forget the details. It can even hamper your getting a second chance at promotion as people will dub you a "sore loser." The less you say, the better for your own mental and political health. Don't kid yourself about friendship with peers. True friendship between competitors is impossible. You would only be giving someone ammunition that could be used against you in the future.

New Interests Help

Find a diversion outside of work. Try something new; become more active socially. Don't go home and brood over your loss. It's up to you to make yourself think about other things. Endless postmortems end up reflected in your face. People can actually see you conducting them.

Start looking at other promotion possibilities within the organization. If people see you treating the loss as a temporary thing, they will not see it as a career knockout, just a setback. Go through the motions even if you're not convinced that there are any other opportunities. It will give all of your peers and your boss a sense of relief to see you recover so quickly and move on. You can then take your time healing in private. Remember that nobody really cares how you feel as long as you don't embarrass them by acting out those feelings.

If you got caught in the "you should want to rise" syndrome even though you don't really feel that way, you're reacting more out of what's expected than out of the way you feel. If you're serious about promotion, however, you will have to do more work and compete more aggressively.

PUBLIC FAILURE

You supported the new advertising campaign that reduced sales. You created a product people couldn't wait not to buy. You supported a subordinate whose failure to do the job turned out to be legendary. You designed a system with enough bugs to keep three programmers working two lifetimes and used thousands of dollars worth of computer time into the bargain. You publicly guaranteed that something wouldn't happen but it did.

At least once in your career, unless Lady Luck's face is frozen in a smile, you are going to fail in some way, in a way known or knowable to many people in your organization, your city, or your industry. Despite the many laudable uses of trade and professional associations, they do spread all the news, good and bad. Members you know may be inclined to give you the benefit of the doubt, but the news will go out anyway.

Your failure could be the result of any number of causes. It may have been a miscalculation; you examined the problem and your analysis was off. Result: you are held responsible for an error. You may have made a reasonable decision based on valid assumptions, later rendered invalid. You may have gambled and lost. You may be the scapegoat for someone with more power.

What do you do now? How much damage has your career sustained? Should you stay where you are and try to repair your tarnished image or should you move on and pretend the whole thing never happened?

Cases in Public Failure

Allen and Joyce were in charge of developing a new distribution system for a small, but growing, manufacturer. They began working in early 1978 and made their plans based on a 10 percent inflation rate. Just as the company was prepared to implement the plan, inflation climbed to 12 and then to 14 percent; a 15 to 18 percent increase was predicted. The principal railroad in the plan began to talk of cutting some of the routes they needed. The boss blamed Allen and Joyce. To make matters worse, they had trumpeted their system out before a trade association meeting; now the trade press reported that the whole plan had been scrapped due to "miscalculation." Allen bailed out immediately and took a job 1,500 miles away. Joyce decided to stay and see if anything could be salvaged.

Peter put all of his influence behind a new marketing plan that he believed would bail a natural foods distributor out of its sales doldrums. The plan seemed to be working until it was discovered that a competitor was using practically the same theme aimed at the same target groups. Even though the plan worked, the client was furious. Peter realized that his research had been spotty at best and that he'd been winging it. Both his boss and the client were quick to hold him totally responsible for the embarrassment. They questioned his every idea and action from then on.

Angela had been in line for promotion to department manager until she had an avoidable dispute with Jenny, the dean of the company's secretaries. Since one competent secretary is worth roughly two middle managers, Angela's career was scorched. Jenny carried tales of Angela's lack of maturity to the troops. Her promotion was put on the back burner.

Jeff had the field audit under firm control until two staff people quit and another became ill and missed work for three weeks. As the audit fell farther behind and the partner in charge spent more time at the client's, Jeff could see his prospects for partnership fading.

Are You Facing the Last Conference?

Most important in a public failure is finding out if you're in danger of being fired. If you are, you'll want to act quickly. You may as well find another job before you're done in. There's a big difference between the real threat of being fired and mere embarrassment and temporary ostracism. How tight is your hold on the job?

You can usually tell if you're in danger of being fired immediately in one of three ways: 1) you are isolated from your boss and peers and don't hear the ordinary gossip going through the grapevine; 2) your internal information network reports that successors are being sought or groomed; or 3) you have a gut feeling that being fired is to be your fate.

If your hold on your job is fairly secure, what can you do to salvage any part of the project; smooth over any people problems; or mitigate the damage already done? Before you try to repair the damage either to your pride or your reputation, you've got to try to get your work back on course. Sometimes it's impossible—the thing is a total wipe. If that's the case, don't try to resurrect the project; give it a decent burial and get on to the next job.

Sitting Duck?

Were you a victim? If you were successful in that role, you're likely to get other chances. It is not easy to find a good victim these days. Once you establish yourself as a winner at losing, you will not lack for opportunities. If you were a victim and someone else's scapegoat, who and why? Certain organizations seem to have a collective obsession for finding a final resting place for every great and small problem. No failure goes unassigned, whether it's drunks at the Christmas cocktail party or red ink on the balance sheet.

These organizations are especially delighted to find willing victims in their never-ending quest for scapegoats. The search usually follows a pattern, as does the attributing of blame. Rule: the higher the level of the person who victimized you, the less damage will have been done to your career. This is true in most organizations because people more than one or two levels above you in the hierarchy really don't know you well enough to convincingly portray you as the goat. A top person picking on someone several levels below him or her is almost always thought unsporting. You will be seen by boss and peers as a victim. However, if your boss victimizes you, you're in genuine trouble. He or she does know you well enough in most cases not only to force you to take the blame but also to make you look authentically guilty.

Before you decide whether you'll stay or go or what you'll say and to whom, a quick review is in order. What did happen? Is there any explanation, any reason, for what happened? Forget excuses. "I overlooked that" and "I'm sorry, it won't happen again" are simply excuses. An explanation meets one test: it does not deal in random feelings or gut responses. There is a reconstructable sequence of events. Without that, you've got excuses. Unless you can point to some definitive reason for the failure, you're involved in heart-to-heart recriminations.

Still Cringing

How monumental is your failure? Forget what your boss, peers, or subordinates are saying and the ways in which they are individually and collectively judging you. How do you judge yourself? Until you've decided how bad the incident was, you can't talk about it intelligently, let alone make any reasonable career decisions. For example, the client

was both horrified and furious to see himself mis-
quoted in the *Wall Street Journal* and the name of
the company misspelled. However, he's getting a lot
of publicity that's both accurate and favorable. The
fact that it's his favorite newspaper may have led to
a certain overreaction on his part. This may be
smoothed over as he sees the good results. One error
hasn't killed the effect. One the other hand, if a very
big story has been botched, you may feel differently,
particularly if the error was preventable. In such a
case, you must question your own competence, attention to detail, and the level of service you're
providing. Forget formal performance appraisals;
the only important one is the one you do yourself.

The reason for this self-examination should be
clear. If you are convinced that you've suffered the
ultimate failure short of being indicted for embezzlement, you should pack it in right now and begin
looking for a new job. Although your colleagues
may forgive and forget you won't be able to do
either. If you're going to die of embarrassment, do it
elsewhere.

At this point, there is always someone who begins
the familiar story about false accusation. He or she
can prove, in court or in the newspaper, that it was
someone else's fault. The company has the facts
wrong. He or she is an innocent victim of misunderstanding. Forget all that. If you are seen as guilty,
don't try to establish your innocence; get on with
repairing the damage. Organizational life is not a
court of law. Nobody is tried and found innocent

and tried and found guilty. Judgments are based on a variety of rational and completely irrational grounds. If you try to seek justice in organizational life, you will move further and further from reality toward fantasy. Besides, what difference would justice make? People are still going to judge you according to their perceptions and not objective facts.

For our purposes, and barring having been accused of a concrete crime—embezzlement, being drunk and disorderly at the annual golf outing, or having the client finger you as the sole perpetrator of a major debacle—the unvarnished truth of any situation is of academic interest only. Unless you're writing a book, crave futile but soul-satisfying vindication, or are terribly young and naive, you'd be better off getting on with reshaping and rehabilitating your reputation. This is especially important if the grapevine reports some haziness as to the exact identity of the disgraced one. People may not really be sure it was you. This is often lost on people in a difficult situation. Someone who thinks you're getting a bad deal may simply refuse to pass the rumor on, thereby effectively limiting its circulation.

Even if you decide to try for public vindication or to explain how you made your mistakes, work at your self-analysis. There is always the danger that having made one error, especially an error in judgment, you will make more. Your career can certainly withstand one public failure, even a messy, long-lasting one, but two or three would test anyone's resilience.

20/20 Hindsight Helps

What should you or could you have done to prevent the outcome that upset everybody? Is hindsight really just wishful thinking? Don't overdo by trying to learn something from every mistake. There is such a thing as bad luck. However, get a second opinion. Give the facts, as you know them, to an impartial person who knows neither you nor the organization very well. See what insights that person has. He or she may be able to point out areas in which you may have miscalculated. This same critic may also give you a different perspective on why people are upset. You may have missed a key element. For instance, if you're smarting because a product was three weeks late, you may be surprsied to learn that others are not upset about it. The real problem may be that no one had advance warning that there *was* a lateness problem.

Sometimes the mistake you made is as simple and easy to find as it is devastating. It may even have been something you would do again under the same circumstances. If so, forget the soul searching. It may be a style of doing something that you can't or don't want to change. Mistakes that stem from the personality or workstyle of an individual are always the most difficult to correct and prevent in the future. For example, if your personal style is bluntness and a client likes news of the location of the toilet facilities delivered with tact and feeling, you would have to change your style completely to prevent all future errors. If that's where you've been caught, you may want to think about a different job with a different kind of organization.

Assuming that you have no interest in either a job or career change right now, how can you recover in your present job? By *recover* we mean reestablish any damaged working relationships, gather up any power reins that may have gotten away, and get on with the job. One of the problems with a public failure is the tendency for your boss or his or her boss not to trust you as completely as before. This may be only temporary, but it could interfere with your ability to do the job. If working relationships are so disturbed that your peers are reluctant to cooperate as fully as they once did or so that they won't go overboard again to bail you out, the situation is probably not going to mend. Peers can cause you to fail by refusing to give anything but formal cooperation. Most people need and depend on wholehearted backup rather than mere lip service.

To decide if you can recover, you'll have to assess, one by one, all of the people whose cooperation is vital to you if you are to do your job. If any link in this chain is broken or if all have been weakened, you should rethink staying. For instance, if you depend on the informal information network to help you stay on top of the job, being cut out of the network is fatal. Such a tactic is sometimes used deliberately to force someone out of a job.

Where Are the Bodies?

Hand in hand with your self-analysis should be an attempt to discover the fate or punishment of those who failed publicly in the past. If they were returned to full inner-circle membership and peer cooperation after a certain period, you may be all right. Try to find survivors. The grapevine should already be comparing your real or projected fate with that of some of these people. You might as well see if this information has any predictive value.

The anxiety that pops up most often with public failure centers on the long-range consequences. What are these likely to be and what, if anything, can be done to mitigate them? Most people are prepared for a certain period of political exclusion following failure. What drives them to distraction is the uncertainty—how long will ostracism last? Unless you can do some pretesting or make some judgments based on what happened in the past, you may have to endure the long run in order to know what it will be like. This is a very risky strategy because you can't predict the length of the long run.

Before you abandon the field, keep in mind that most people stay at a job for less than three years. The long run may be five years. Once there has been a complete turnover in bosses, peers, and subordinates, the failure is dead. There will, of course, always be one old-timer who's been there for forty years and remembers every transgression in minute detail. He or she may be listened to on occasion but unless peers can back up the story from some personal recollection his or her influence is lessened.

This is not true of nonprofit organizations where many employees tend to stay for ten or fifteen years. Failures die harder in such an environment.

You've got to learn the level of tolerance of your particular political climate. Don't kid yourself. If you think you're prey to the long-memory syndrome, change jobs or be prepared to have your future successes share the limelight with the remembered failure.

The Last Roundup

What is a postmortem with your boss or some reasonably non-competitive peer worth? It's a risk, but it might give you vital information about what others see as the damage to your career. This is something you'll want to consider very carefully. A rule of thumb on postmortems is that they should be conducted only after as many of the facts as possible have been revealed and when there is no chance of changing the outcome of whatever mistake you're autopsying. If there's any possibility of change of outcome, hold off.

Should you try for an oral or written postmortem? If you want a more candid appraisal, go for the oral postmortem. If you want the official line (one someone is willing to express in writing), try to put your ideas in writing first and get a written response. This allows you to shape the facts or use them selectively. If your boss does not disagree with your analysis but responds on the basis of the facts you used, he or she is playing in your backyard. You'd want a written response only if you want to commit your boss to a position. This may be rather difficult, if not impossible, to accomplish. A boss trying to securely fasten the blame for a serious error will go for the written analysis, but may initiate it independently. If the blame can't be firmly fixed on you, the analysis will probably be oral. Some bosses won't talk at all. They'll skirt the issues by stating that "there's no point in dredging up all of that again," or they'll respond with the cliché "Let sleeping dogs lie." The problem is that you may need to know the species of dog that is sleeping. Peers may be helpful in determining the species, since it's doubtful that the boss kept his or her view totally private.

If you can't get anything out of anybody, it may be time to grab the initiative and write your analysis of what happened. Be careful not to imply blame or to shift it from yourself. Your analysis should read like a newspaper account of a fire. If you don't stick to verifiable facts, the only response you'll get will be a defensive one. You want to use your analysis to test the waters, to flush out any alternate opinions. One of the dangers in going the memo-with-copies route is that you may discover that very few people have an understanding of what happened or who was responsible. Until you ascertain the number of people in your organization who know that there's been a public failure and that you were involved, don't put anything in writing that can or may be widely circulated. You can indict and convict yourself in writing in front of people who didn't know that a crime had been committed.

Some of your peers are plugged into different networks than you are. Seek their counsel. You may have to trade some of the facts of what happened to secure their cooperation, but they are your best hope of learning how widely circulated has been the news of the debacle. If their nets don't snare any reasonably accurate rumors, you'll have a very important piece of information; one or a number of people are conspiring to keep the whole incident under wraps. That's good news. Somebody (or several somebodies) has decided you are not to be sacrificed.

Only Everybody Knows

Suppose your whole sad story is widely known, not to everybody, just to everybody with any power. Are you getting any sympathy or comfort from people, or are you being ignored and isolated? If your sympathy level is so low as to be imperceptible, especially from those above you, that's a bad sign. Your enemies may dance in the corridors, but the neutrals should offer at least some sign of empathy. If that doesn't happen, it's a very bad sign. The word is out, even at a nonverbal level, that you are out. If that's the situation, it's résumé time. Don't wait until this has been going on for months before you act. Doing so just reduces your self-confidence, something you'll need for your job search.

Do you have any allies or are you judged to be in so deep politically that your allies have totally faded away? If you can't point to a single peer who feels that you are still worth cooperating with and who still sees you as a serious competitor, it's probably because you've been written off. "Poor Margie, she's really beyond the pale."

Over the Roadblocks

Is it possible for your boss and peers to put barriers between you and people with whom you must interact in order to get your work done? Has this happened? No one likes to be seen with a loser, particularly if the disaster is not well understood but seen as a megaevent. Still, if it's your boss or peers who are keeping others from cooperating, it's a sign that they have lost confidence in your ability to do the job. They are worried about what fresh disasters await. They may be scrambling to replace you before you err again.

What had your reputation been before you had your public disaster? If you'd always been thought competent, this one problem may be awful, but as ultimately short-lived as falling downstairs in public. People look at patterns. If they judge this failure to be an isolated incident, your predisaster reputation was probably very good. Beware the tendency to cast yourself as a victim. There's not as much sympathy for victims as you'd think. The leap from being a victim of others to self-victimization is quite short. Don't point the way.

Ultimately we come to the big issue: how do you measure career damage? There are three important clues, but no one foolproof formula. 1) What was your relationship with your boss before the debacle? The less secure and easy that relationship, the more damage may have been done. You should have some feelings about that relationship. 2) Was any permanent harm done to the organization's bottom line, or is it more a case of temporary, though acute, embarrassment? 3) How well plugged in politically are you to levels about your boss and to peers on your boss's level?

Lukewarm and Cooling

If your boss was lukewarm about you before, you're probably through. If he or she was a strong, even enthusiastic supporter, you'll probably be able to find your way back into favor. If you don't know for sure, assume the worst, because the fact that you don't know means the worst has already happened. It's part of your job to be able to predict your boss's reaction. If you really want an oral assessment of your future, ask for either a raise or a promotion and listen to how the request is treated instead of to what the response is. If the question arouses anger, you should begin updating your résumé; if it calls forth surprise and some dismay, you may survive.

If, all wishful thinking aside, your future is not

completely destroyed with the organization, you should put every effort into generating a quick, highly visible success. This success should be something that you can publicize through the internal grapevine, through the trade and community press, and through memos to your superiors.

The success does not have to be of equal weight with your failure. The most important thing is that it be very easy to spot. People must be able to see that you did something well and that others reacted favorably. There are two ways in which you can do something in, say, three to six weeks that will help diffuse the negative gossip in the grapevine by replacing it with positive information.

The first is the easiest to arrange. Agree to head up a volunteer activity outside of work that will generate a lot of publicity. Even though you may find it appalling to badger inflation's victims for money, this is the time to squelch those feelings and work very hard pressing people to give. Remember, you're doing this not solely for a noble cause but also to get favorable publicity for yourself. You're "using" the volunteer organizaton, of course, but in this era of reluctant givers and high inflation people are likely to overlook your motives and help you get publicity if you produce. Successful money-raising campaigns often get good press coverage.

Are you going to count on people at work seeing the newspaper publicity? Not a chance. Write a memo to your boss informing him or her of your role as chief fundraiser, chairperson, whatever, and then keep him or her posted as you blaze a trail. This is a lot of work, but how much is a quick, visible success worth if it means restoring some aura of success to your reputation? Don't get involved if you can't do this with some sincerity. Raise funds for your alumni association if that's more palatable. Be sure the fund raising is an adult activity so that you can build business contacts in case you need to change jobs unexpectedly. Community-wide noncontroversial activities that generate broad public support are best.

If there's nothing in which you can get immediately involved, look for the most thankless but possible job you can volunteer for at work. What does your boss really hate to do? If it's soliciting subordinates for contributions to charity, volunteer to do so on your own time, not when you should be working at your job. Your boss will know why you're volunteering, but so what? You're trying to smooth things over and what's wrong with that?

Suppose you have done everything you can think of, plus ten things suggested by your most imaginative friends, and you're still beyond the pale. Move on. Being an outcast for a few weeks or even months may be tolerable; after that your morale and even your ability to do your job will falter. Once the organization, collectively and individually, has decided you are a loser, it won't take long before you think and act like one. Why put yourself under that kind of stress? There are plenty of other organizations where you can be productive. Leave this situation before you develop serious doubts about your own abilities. Don't hang around if things can't be mended. Martyrs are the most unattractive species in organizational life. Get on with your career somewhere else, storing away anything that you have learned from this situation.

As you move on, resolve never to discuss the dreary story in loving detail with new associates. You wouldn't print negative stories about yourself in the company newsletter; why discuss them? If you perform well and your new colleagues hear rumors about the problems in your old shop, they may charge them off to sour grapes that a star such as yourself got away.

Second, resolve to keep active in your trade and professional associations so that if some other disaster happens you'll know enough people to counter bad publicity and to give you plenty of instant job-hunting contacts. The only insurance you can take out against public disasters is knowing and being favorably known by a large number of people. Then, if something does happen, a large number of people will think it couldn't have been your fault or, best of all, they'll like and respect you anyway. That's career nirvana.

Chapter 9

The Killer Bs: Blockage, Boredom, and Burnout

Some job conditions would cause anybody to run home and put all his or her savings into lottery tickets in the hope that a big win would eliminate wage slavery forever. Sometimes these conditions are obvious: no heat, sexual harassment, no key to the executive washroom, low salary, overwork, not enough work.

Sometimes they're not so obvious. You may feel uncomfortable without realizing why. It may be the structure of the job, career problems that lessen concentration, or simply demands that can't be met. These problems are no less important to the work theater or to you than the obvious ones. They can be even more deadly. That's why this chapter is called the Killer Bs.

Blockage, boredom, and burnout all deserve attention, planning, and action. Each is sometimes misidentified because each looks and feels very much like depression and job dissatisfaction. Check yourself from time to time to make sure you're not infected with any of these. If you are, take steps to get back on the right track.

BLOCKAGE: ALL GEARED UP, NO PLACE TO GO

"What we've got here is a young management team full of sparkle, fresh ideas, ready to go," the president said. "That's how we stay ahead of the competition." Wonderful as that myth may seem, much as both the president and management team would like to believe that youth is a magical elixir, there is a problem. A young management team, without a balance of some older and some younger managers in the hierarchy, means that there will inevitably be either a great many opportunities at one time for people to move up or to be hired from outside, or none at all. That approach means feast or famine and a certain lack of organizational stability. Lack of internal movement will be a problem for those who like the organization and want to stay there. Those who don't like the organization's style will move on.

The Nursery

When Gina went to work for the advertising

agency, she had no illusions that she'd find many geriatric ward candidates in the upper ranks. In fact, the president of the agency was forty-two the creative group vice president was thirty-eight. What she failed to realize initially was that her own supervisor was barely two years older than she. After two years, a much more thorough study of the hierarchy, and some discreet inquiries, she realized that all the vice presidents and senior supervisors were under forty. At thirty-two, she saw herself as having to wait for years before she could move up because the people ahead of her had settled in for the duration.

Gina's best hope was that someone would be seduced by another agency, thus creating an opening, or, next best, pull a Gauguin and retire to the Missouri Ozarks to raise apples.

As the president had promised, her colleagues were young, full of fresh ideas, and robustly healthy. Gina was meeting one of the most frustrating, yet widespread career knockouts—blockage.

Blockage means that whatever is supposed to move doesn't. In organizations, blockage means that each job, regardless of title or relative level, is a dead-end job. Because everyone is so close in age, no openings are created by retirement or any of the health problems that normally plague the over-fifty crowd. The only openings are those resulting from people moving out of the organization. Blockage is intensified if top management also has equity in the firm. Why should they leave?

We Like It

Blockage doesn't just happen. In most organizations it comes about as a result of deliberate management philosophy. Either they get rid of anyone over fifty or they simply never allow anyone who isn't an owner to remain until he or she reaches fifty; thus the organization tilts heavily toward the underforty average. Because nobody is in any danger of retirement or death from old age, there is virtually no movement up the ranks. You have a better chance of getting a high level job as an outsider than as an insider moving up from within. A strong indicator of blockage in a company is the lack of a retirement plan. If you're a copy supervisor at thirty-two and your supervisor is thirty-five and his or her manager is forty, your chances of movement within the organization while still in your thirties are fairly slim. You're much more likely to get tired of waiting and move on.

Another aspect of blockage is that it produces a crisis atmosphere. There are always new people who don't know what's been done in the past. The lack of an oral history or tradition keeps everybody busy repeating what was done before, both successes and failures.

There are two kinds of blockage. The kind described so far is the kind in which the whole management team is young and the only movement is out of the organization with replacement by someone at the same level. The organization has been set up so that promotion from within is almost impossible.

The second kind is less often identified because what people say is at variance with what they do. In these organizations, everyone seems on a fast track, but some of the people have decided that they have gotten as far as they can or want to go. They appear to have a straight shot at the top even though they or their bosses have decided that they're not going any further. This kind of blockage, given the protective coloring of the people, is harder to see. There are few people in their thirties, regardless of what they tell themselves, who tell peers and superiors that they're planning to stay in a job until death or retirement.

Since the accent-on-youth companies inevitably attract ambitious candidates, identifying the particular kind of blockage that exists is a problem. Most of the people who apply to, or are recruited into, such companies are there because they're encouraged by the relative youth of those holding the position they want. "Just look how far Freddy has gone, and he's only thirty-five." Often they forget to ask the obvious questions, if Freddy is a vice president at thirty-five, how old is his boss? If the boss is forty, how will Freddy get his boss's job? Most important, is Freddy really hoping or expecting to move up?

Kill, Don't Cooperate

Blockage promotes destructive office politics. Efforts turn from cooperation to get the job done to plans to discredit or force out internal competitors. The homogeneous age group means that everybody has similar views of how things should be done. In some organizations, the whole management team seems to have been cloned from the president; the president's work-style (sometimes even lifestyle) seems to be the one approved style. Every mistake, every deviation will be noted because, with so much conformity, the least difference appears monumental.

Age, of course, isn't the only important aspect of promotion patterns. Has there been a complete turnover in management? What happened to the older people who left? This is especially relevant in five- to ten-year-old start-up companies. The owner may have started the business as a thirty- or thirty-five-year-old. Younger employees who weren't promoted in a short time left. They realized fairly quickly that they had no chance unless their own bosses recognized the blockage; and the blockage was just too much for them to tolerate. Vacancies created by these departures were filled with more young people.

There is an organizational advantage to blockage of this kind. No employee's salary will increase solely from longevity. That means that even with an adjustment for inflation, salaries remain fairly constant. This is true even though salaries for personnel replacing those who leave will continue to rise.

Short-term Only

There are organizational disadvantages to blockage. First, since none of the newly hired young people are likely to see the job as more than a way station to something better, there's no long-term commitment in the ranks of middle managers. Second, word soon gets out that a company has a blockage problem. There is reluctance to dig in and become fully involved with such firms. The accent on youth disturbs and depresses the forty- to forty-five-year-old. He or she begins to look for another job. Fearing the arrival of his or her fiftieth birthday, the individual becomes somewhat frantic in seeking a new position. This is true even if the person's job is in no danger. The fear is that any mistake made will be attributed to aging.

Secretaries and administrators may soon be the longest-term employees, which gives them disproportionate power. They are the ones who will train the continuing flow of young managers joining the organization. This means that the job viewpoint is conditioned by people who have never held the job. Support personnel have become keepers of the organization's traditions; they now have the power to reshape them as they pass them on. No middle manager may have been with the firm long enough to challenge this.

But what of the worker who finds himself or herself in such a situation? Blockage is often an insidious problem for the ambitious manager because he or she gets conflicting signals. Surely this is a fast-track organization. There are no fifty-plus senior level people. Some of the younger managers have probably been promoted in the past. Maybe this particular employee will be lucky and join their ranks. There is a reluctance to leave until the manager is absolutely certain that his or her boss is going to stay and that no other opportunity will open up.

Wait or Bolt

Faced with this problem, many people decide to wait it out indefinitely, often with neither grace nor patience, or they get discouraged and leave. In boom times, this is the classic pattern; in recessions, this may not be so easy. Some organizations delay the effects of blockage by expanding horizontally. This gives the appearance of movement. In the 1980s, this is not going to be a likely solution.

If someone who's currently a victim of blockage gets another job, how sure can he or she be that the blockage problem wouldn't be waiting at the next firm? Part of the reason why so many firms have a blockage problem is the postwar baby boom. The baby boomers, who are in the same general age group, are at about the same level in most organizations, and there are huge numbers of them. A few have moved ahead of their peers, but that doesn't change circumstances for the rest.

Suppose you are stuck. Of course, you could start

looking for another job, make new contacts, etc., but, for a variety of reasons, you don't want to do so. You may have priorities in your personal life that demand your energy. You may enjoy the people with whom you work or the work you do. You may be extremely well paid for the amount you must produce. Whatever your reasons, you don't want to make a change now. How can you make blockage work for you?

How can you turn the twin characteristics of no room at the top and a fairly rapid turnover to your advantage? What can you do to ensure that you'll be in a favorable position when you finally are ready to leave or when a real opportunity to advance opens up? Your best strategy will be to make as many horizontal moves as you can. Become a generalist by performing different jobs or by managing two or three departments at your level. If you are managing customer service now, why not get into the direct mail end of the business or into advertising next? Consider this an educational opportunity for which the firm will pay you. If you eventually decide to move to another organization, especially a larger one, you'll find that your varied background gives you a competitive advantage. Your peers are trying to perfect their skills in a particular area rather than broaden their experience. You cannot help but have an advantage if you've functioned effectively in different areas.

Blockage is a major career knockout because it encourages people to focus solely on the upward mobility aspect of a job. Instead of looking for a way to make the time until you're ready to change productive, you become the victim of your own discontent. This lowers your productivity and keeps you from profiting fom the available opportunities.

Your career is only temporarily blocked. The company has not decided that you're unpromotable. It's simply not set up to encourage promotion from within. Therefore, by focusing on blockage you are refusing to accept the intrinsic nature of the organization. You are trying to change what is, by design, unchangeable. With such an attitude, your productivity will suffer over a two- or three-year period. Your resentment and frustration are going to be clear to any but the most casual observer. If you become that frustrated, leave. If not, use the opportunity given you to practice your political skills and diversify your job experience.

One of the things organizations with blockage are never given credit for is that of being breeding grounds for truly broadly based management consultants. If it is your long-term goal to be a management consultant, here's your chance to practice the skills you'll need. In an organization without blockage, you'd eventually become a specialist in one area as you move up the corporate ladder. That's fine if that's your career goal. Perhaps it's your goal only because you can't see the other possibilities, those that diversity offers.

A favorite myth of fast trackers is that there's great significance to holding the same job for three to five years; the company feels you're unworthy to move up or a future employer may think the company judged you in this manner. If you allow your career to be guided by what a friend told you happened to a friend of his, you are basing your decisions on the least possible available evidence. Would you buy a stock based on a hot tip you overheard in a lunchroom? Why base your career on the same kind of information?

There are as many employer attitudes toward upward mobility as there are employers. You will always be out of sync for some employers and in sync for others. You cannot make a valid generalization over time for large organizations, probably not even for small ones. Even start-up organizations can change. It's very difficult to stand one's ground as business conditions have changed enough to require a change in personnel philosophy.

The final fact to keep in mind is that, if top management of a company ages and moves into its collective fifties and sixties, the accent on youth will change. It's very difficult to stand one's ground as firmly in favor of the under-forty crowd as one creeps toward sixty. You should have only two concerns as a blocked employee. Can you wait it out? Will it be worth your while to do so? The younger top management is, the more concerned you'll be about blockage. If top management is between forty-five and fifty, it's a gray area. If top management is over fifty, the whole complexion and philosophy of the organization may change rapidly.

BOREDOM: WHEN THE JOB'S NO CHALLENGE

One journalism professor keeps goading his students to greater effort by reminding them that "there are no boring subjects, just boring writers." To an extent, this is also true of most professional, technical, and even clerical jobs. Yet, one of the most common complaints of working people is how boring their jobs are. Boredom can lead to job termination, career reversal, and desperation.

Boredom means dullness, repetition, routine, structure that's confining, tradition, no room in which to move around, lack of opportunity for experimentation; in other words, it has all the attributes of sameness. Surprisingly, boredom has nothing to do with a person's age or length of time on the job. People can become bored and unmotivated after a month or it might not happen for twenty years.

Is It Catching?

Boredom is a major career knockout because bosses tend to see bored employees as infected with a contagious disease that may spread to otherwise satisfied people. This misconception is held by many employers. Sitting on either side of someone in the throes of terminal boredom may be two productive, enthusiastic, turned-on people who think they are doing something wonderfully interesting. Faced with their neighbor's boredom, they are forced to define their own attitudes. Even if the bored one tells them why he or she is bored, they're likely to see this as his or her problem, as something totally extraneous to their feelings about what they are doing.

Several bored people in a department, however, can infect others. One person may be out of step, but two or more are harbingers. They are also more likely to publicize their feelings more widely since they have the courage of company.

Some bosses see boredom as a character weakness. "The trouble with Jessie is that she just doesn't know how to handle her work. She's always so bored. It must be that she's unrealistic, or maybe just naive."

As usual, our interests are not identical with the employer's. We're concerned with boredom as a worker problem. What impact does it have on an individual's career?

If people could mask all signs of boredom, remain quietly bored, even yawn occasionally as they get on with the job, boredom would be a fairly minor problem. After all, about 80 percent of the work in any job is routine; only 20 percent is what might be called creative. This seems to be true whether you're a skydiver, president of an organization, or somebody's assistant. Some job boredom is inevitable and no big deal. But that's not the kind of boredom we're talking about.

The boredom we're talking about has a devastating impact on productivity, self-motivation, office relations; it may ultimately lead to being fired and getting a very bad reference. In fact, this kind of boredom is inseparable from declining motivation. Once someone has decided he or she is bored, self-motivation ceases. Outside motivation, threats or flattery, won't work unless these techniques address the boredom problem. When someone is truly bored, all of his or her other hot buttons are on "off."

Who's at Fault?

Bosses are very sensitive to worker boredom. A visibly bored worker calls attention not only to his or her own shortcomings but to implied shortcomings in the organization and the boss. If someone is bored, a boss has failed either by not providing stimulating work or by not restructuring the job to eliminate the problem. Boredom is an implicit criticism of the boss. That's the real issue. It's hard to be bored invisibly by oneself. Boredom can't be allowed to exist. It has to be rooted out before other employees begin examining their jobs. Firing and boredom have a very special relationship. The more boring the boss thinks the jobs his subordinates have, the quicker the action to get rid of anyone who reflects this hidden assessment.

Firing is the common cure for boredom—even though nobody may be fired because he or she is bored per se. Reasons given may include "personality conflicts," "not performing up to par," and all the catch phrases used to cover any kind of attitude problem. Performance may in fact have declined to an unacceptable level. If so, firing can be justified as being for cause. Still, the bored person, unproductive or not, is being fired for having expressed his or her boredom, not just for failure to perform.

Next to firing, the most common way of dealing with boredom is to grant transfers. It's widely believed that movement, any kind of movement, would eliminate the problem. If the employee has always been productive and liked by his superiors, transfer is seen as a "second chance" for the individual to straighten out. Sometimes, if there's enough thought or just plain luck in the transfer process, this works.

From the worker's point of view, boredom feels like a gradual slowing down. It doesn't always have a direct effect on the individual's energy level. Someone bored mindless might run around to rearrange papers, furniture, or people, all at a terrifying rate, accomplishing nothing. When a high-energy person gets bored, activity increases; in a low-energy person, activity decreases.

Boredom is seldom the result of lack of work, though many people think so. That's a simplistic explanation. Based on self-analysis, people fired because of boredom listed the following principal causes for their problem.

1. "I've changed and the job hasn't. There was plenty of work to do and decent conditions in which to do it. The problem was that I was no longer

interested in or compatible with the work. I wanted to grow in a completely different direction. It was impossible to do so in that job, so I simply stopped trying."

2. **"There was no room for any kind of individual decision making.** The job was so tightly structured that there were even scripts to memorize with appropriate responses to questions in customer conversations. I became a robot."

3. **"My boss insisted on making all the decisions. I** was left to choose between lined and unlined paper. I had no reason to try because I could make no independent decisions of any significance."

4. **"The job was supposed to lead to a better job.** Instead, I got trapped in the entry level position while all around me people moved up or out."

5. **"I was so hopelessly overqualified for the job it was embarrassing.** A not very bright secretary could have performed admirably, but the boss liked to be surrounded by MBAs from good schools."

6. **"The job never really existed.** The spot needed to be filled because it was in the budget or to provide prestige for the boss by increasing his staff, or to hold the position while the job develops or some other reason that requires a warm body but not necessarily a mind."

7. **"We did the same things in the same way until I thought I would drown in a combination of tedium**

and resentment. I worked with the same four people for five years. I could predict how each one would react in any situation. There were no surprises."

The common theme in the explanations is that boredom is a response. Unable to make any changes in either the style or the content of the job, the worker turned his or her total attention to hanging on. Productivity became a pawn. One of the ways people fought their boredom was to spend as much time as possible going through the motions without actually accomplishing anything. They were getting back at the organization that was causing them such great discomfort. Self-righteous to a fault, many bored workers talked in terms of effort. They skipped any discussion of the results of that effort. In truth, nothing was accomplished.

So it looks like a good old-fashioned guerrilla action on the part of the employee. As long as Dick doesn't get caught, he can create his own excitement and thus divert attention from the real problem. The more Dick needs the job, the more likely this is to happen.

It was actually a step forward for him to recognize that he was bored. Many people fail to identify boredom as a cause of the problems they are having. The harder it is to measure productivity, the more likely people are to forget about it altogether until there's a major crisis.

Up to this point it's the organization that's taking it on the chin, but that's just a superficial analysis.

What really happens to bored workers is that they begin to doubt their own competence. That's the career killer.

Boredom starts with the individual's self-knowledge that he or she is definitely bored. The second stage is a striking out, almost an attempt to sabotage the organization by withholding services or by merely going through the motions. The third stage is the beginning of a realization that maybe he or she is not really that capable, maybe it's important to hold on to this job. Finally, the worker begins to doubt that he or she can get another job or be productive anywhere. The minute this happens all of the signs of internal struggle pop out. At that point, the organization has usually recognized the worker's lack of effectiveness and taken some action.

Angst or Action

All of the suffering that people experience before the organization acts—and in some organizations this can take years—is quite unnecessary. Once you know that you're bored, it's up to you, the individual, to protect your own career. *It's your problem.* Nobody else really cares, nor can anybody help until your job is in danger because you won't do the work.

There are a number of actions you can take to revive interest in your present job, if only to grant you the time you need to look for a new one. Remember, if you are fired for cause, your reference as well as your self-esteem may be compromised. So, do something about your boredom. Begin by doing what you're supposed to do differently; change the order in which you do your tasks or alter your work time. If that's not possible, ask your boss to add some new duties or reorder the old ones. Since it is your problem, it's up to you to propose, in writing, ways to restructure the job. Decide what would make the work you do less tedious and more interesting. Don't expect a lot of help in thinking through the problem. You'll be better off if your boss is only interested in ratifying what you propose and not in helping you think up the changes.

If the personnel department has job analysts, talk to them. See if there are any openings to which you might transfer. Be careful with the personnel department. If word gets back that you're looking for a transfer, your boss could be piqued. If you don't get a transfer, you could have political problems. In some companies, personnel may protect you, in others it won't. Don't find out the hard way.

Talk to people in your trade or professional organization. What kinds of jobs do they do that you may not have considered? No one set of skills equals a particular job. Determine your skills rather than concentrate on a particular job title. There's a lot of leeway, and you can learn about other jobs by talking to people with similar experience and education.

What's the Real Cause?

Analyze the real source of your boredom. Is it the rigidity of the way the job is structured? Is it repetition? If you cannot handle repetition, you may need to change careers, not just jobs. Is it the fact that you are expected to do some maintenance? Unfortunately, brain surgeons as well as clerks do maintenance. Don't tell yourself that what you need is more variety unless you can give a succinct definition of variety. If you can't finish the sentence. "My idea of great variety is . . .," you're not getting at the problem.

Are you just hanging on? A great many people are too lazy, not motivated enough, or just not eager enough to change jobs. They know this, though it's rare to hear someone say so publicly. If that's what you're doing, forget it. Everybody with any eyesight at all knows how you feel. Your body language screams boredom eight hours a day. Your choice is not between boredom and hanging on, it's between getting a new job and being fired.

Talk to a career counselor or a psychotherapist. If your behavior represents a pattern, e.g., this is the third job on which you've confronted boredom, boredom is probably a symptom of other career problems. Don't try to run up your losing streak. Get help now.

Remember that some job-related boredom is to be expected in every job. There are days when the tedium of routine work will get to the most conscientious worker. It's the pattern of consistent boredom over time that's such a career killer. And, because you are probably on the job at least eight hours a day, it's worth it to do something about boredom.

BURNOUT: THE HIGH COST OF DOING GOOD

In an article in the May 1979 issue of *Psychology Today*, Christina Maslach and Susan E. Jackson described burnout as "a syndrome of emotional exhaustion and cynicism that frequently occurs among individuals who do 'peoplework'—who spend considerable time in close encounters with others under conditions of chronic tension and stress." Their article focused on male police officers and their families and the problems they faced with burnout. But what happens when you invest your whole self in your job and you're not a policeman and something is still wrong?

In the 1980s, it's necessary to expand the definition of burnout to include not just policemen, social workers, and medical people—the obvious choices —but the full range of people who work in service businesses, especially all kinds of nonprofit groups, as well as those in communication jobs, sales, banking, brokerage houses, accounting. In other words, one must include anyone whose job encompasses extensive people contact.

The People Squeezers

There are people whose work with others is strongly conditioned by social assumptions. Because the product you're selling includes a personality, much more is expected. For example, if you buy a blender, you have no personal involvement with the manufacturer. As long as it works properly, you don't care what the manufacturer's attitude toward you the customer is. Not so with those who provide services. From them you expect feeling, caring, and sincerity, even if it's from a kid who's bagging twenty pounds of potatoes with a carton of eggs.

It's not difficult to find doctors and nurses, social workers, paramedics, teachers, and public officials with burnout. But other people who have extensive people contact show symptoms of burnout too. Strictly speaking, they are not engaged in "doing good"; if anything, the Maslach/Jackson definition is not extensive enough because it doesn't cover people whose burnout stems from the need to maintain an attitude, a veneer of interest, that covers the opposite set of emotions. Yet these burnout victims are no less seriously affected than the traditional ones. They are often unaware that they have a problem.

Love Thy Client Sincerely

In a period of robust economic activity, when businesses are expanding and many jobs are available, neither top management nor customers expects each employee to project absolute love of the job or customer at every minute. It is enough that the product or service appear at the proper time and in the proper condition. People are preoccupied with keeping up with demand. In bad times, in a never-ending attempt to satisfy the customer absolutely, leaving no margin for error, the pressure on employees to perform at a consistently high level produces burnout. Fear also plays a part. "If I don't perform perfectly, will I be fired?"

There is a safety factor when the economy is robust because the anxiety employees feel about their jobs is somewhat diminished. With everybody working at top speed, organizations are not as worried about money and the pressure on any one individual to perform under threat of losing his or her job is lessened. There's "give" in the system. Let the economy turn down and the opposite happens. All of a sudden, issues of style, attitude, and behavior become paramount as management scrambles to shore up any weaknesses. The pressure is on.

There is no such thing as a pressure-free or stress-free work environment. No organization is so confident, so protected from competitors and the vagaries of customers, that its employees need never worry about their jobs. However, in times of economic crisis, the pressure increases. That pressure, especially if it is unrelenting, produces burnout in some employees. People in the manufacturing industries also suffer from increased pressure, but there are fewer cases of burnout in manufacturing than there are in the service businesses.

Nobody can hold his or her breath forever. Nobody can perform consistently at exactly the same level every day without some variation. Over time, the felt need to do so produces burnout.

Looking at the Symptoms

There are a great variety of burnout symptoms; they depend on the degree of burnout and on the individual's response to stress. The most common ones are listed here.

1. There is emotional withdrawal from the client or customer. Instead of enthusiasm, the customer or client gets honed-down service devoid of any emotional or human connection. It's not rudeness, anger, or indifference. It's as if the individual were looking at the client's problems from a great distance.

2. There is increased use of alcohol, food, drugs, or whatever the person has used as an emotional crutch or bandage in the past. This is often the employer's first clue that there is a problem.

3. There is a withdrawal from peers, family, and friends. Since they can't understand or may not care what's happening, there's no need to burden them with a lot of random feelings.

4. There's talk of The Great Escape. This may be to a farm without utilities, the South Sea Islands, New York, or simply to an entirely different line of work. The ultimate is to start one's own business; that idea seems to symbolize freedom from pressure and people demands. (In actuality, self-employed people get burnout as often as those who work for others.)

5. There is less patience with family and friends. The person is absorbed with his or her own work-related crises. There is nothing left over emotionally to spend on others. This seems like deliberate coldness rather than self-absorption.

6. There is increasing impatience with preserving outward appearances. That is, there's no desire or even capacity to pretend that work is fun, interesting, or whatever the expected response is. Sometimes people become compulsively honest at the expense of tact and discretion.

7. There is a feeling that the individual can no longer meet work expectations. These seem overwhelming. The person sees himself or herself as working very hard to produce very little.

8. There is physical tiredness and lethargy. Regardless of the number of hours of sleep the individual gets, he or she is always tired.

Burnout is quite a shock to the employers and clients of the victims. The latter especially may become angry when they see the symptoms; they may not understand what is happening.

Having been told to believe that they're entitled, not only to service, but to real concern and feeling from the people who serve them, people are reluctant to settle for anything less. As one nurse said, "My patients want to be sure I really care personally about them as individuals. They have no interest in professional service rendered with a professional attitude. If I don't appear to worry that they won't recover, they think I'm cold and not a very good nurse. I have to feel genuine pain to satisfy my patients." The confusion between love and service seems to be complete in medicine. Although it's less complete in business, it's still there, especially in selling.

Salespeople are expected to like, as well as be liked by, their clients. Even the most cynical, sophisticated client does not hesitate to put his or her relationships with those who sell on a personal basis. "Fred is a great guy and that's why we do business with him. We're even friends outside the office." Maybe, but it's likely that Fred has understood the attitude he is expected to take and, because it works and produces commissions, he takes it.

All of this need to pretend is so at variance with the 1960s philosophy of "doing your own thing" and "letting it all hang out," it's no wonder that some of the graduates of that era find it hard to adjust. In fact, burnout is a growing problem among the twenty-five- to forty-year-old set.

The number of people in the twenty-five to thirty-five crowd who have reorganized their work lives to combat burnout is growing. A typical response has been to work at a job for a few years, then quit or force termination. Using employment compensation and savings, the burnout victim spends from six months to a year pursuing other interests. Then he or she returns to work.

Burnout becomes a real career knockout when an individual realizes that, emotionally, he or she has nothing left to give. Until that point is reached, the symptoms may have been obvious to others but not to the victim. Now it's no longer possible to focus on whether or not one contract gets signed, one patient recovers, or one client is satisfied to the level of his or her expectations. Productivity declines. As one commercial loan officer described his developing problem, "all I had to do was be nice to the company comptroller. He wasn't a bad guy and a biweekly lunch to keep the deal sweet didn't seem like much. The conversation was not brilliant—in fact, it consisted of his talking and my agreeing. After a while, I began to argue. Not about anything very significant, just picking out a point here of there. In three months, I could see the account getting shaky. That's when I went to my boss and asked to be reassigned."

Altogether Now . . . Feel!

The unrelenting external demand to feel the appropriate feeling on cue seems to be the major catalyst leading to burnout in people whose work is people-oriented, even though the feelings do not revolve around life-and-death issues.

Part of the battle fatigue teachers experience has to be the pressure to actually and sincerely care whether each and every student really learns. Professionalism doesn't mean doing the best one can in the appropriate way, it means being emotionally involved. Parents expect teachers to show as much anxiety as they feel if little Susie is falling behind in reading. A teacher who doesn't is a "bad" teacher. This need to extract feeling from teachers has caused many people whose jobs were not in danger from cutbacks to flee for their sanity.

Media people can't genuinely respect the public figures they interview, whether rock stars or politicians, when they're bored to death by people who are too shallow and silly to be taken seriously, yet they have to play along. These people frequently demand uncritical admiration as the price of the interview. If you don't go along, you may not get the story.

Burnout victims share one common trait. They are so emotionally drained, so apathetic, that they can no longer feel much of anything, professionally or personally. They have usually reached either a crisis or an emotional bottom. However, burnout does have a cycle and there is a way back.

Stress and Pressure

The burnout cycle usually starts as stress. You're under pressure to perform at a specific level. The problem is that your performance is not to have peaks and valleys, it's to be sustained at the same high level over a fairly long period of time. This may be explained as consistency. It's not realistic or possible to motivate oneself to work at exactly the same level of intensity every day, day after day, but no employer is going to admit this.

Medical people learned this long ago; the ones who are in for the stretch have learned to distance themselves emotionally to a degree, to provide outlets other than medicine that take them out of their own life-and-death concerns, and to create their own support groups of colleagues up against the same problems. These support groups may not be formally organized as such but they are there to reinforce the individual's job performance and to stave off the cynicism.

One of the reasons hospital nurses tend to burn out very quickly is that they have problems with both personal detachment from patients (not taught well at all in nursing schools) and social expectations. If they are always to assist the healing process, they have to be virtually superhuman.

Much of what is diagnosed as career change amounts to running away from the emotional intensity demanded by a particular kind of job or industry. Many schoolteachers and professors who leave education leave, not from fear of unemployment, but because of the realization that they have burned out, have used up their emotional reserves and are no longer able to do the job properly. Flight seems the only possibility.

Not everybody in a high-intensity job suffers burnout. Some of the people doing these jobs seem to understand instinctively how to pace themselves; they give just so much of themselves and no more. The more idealistic you are, the more you believe in what you do, the more likely you are to have at least

217

some of the symptoms of burnout. Fervor breeds burnout. It's not necessary to be disenchanted with what you do to burn out; you can love your job and still develop the symptoms. There are emotional overloads even in love affairs.

Performance Declines

Burnout has a tremendous and, to the employer, inexplicable impact on performance. No boss really understands how, when you've been doing so well, your performance can deteriorate so suddenly. You begin to be apathetic, detached, drained, unenthusiastic, and altogether less able to perform well. If you no longer get a sense of accomplishment from what you do or no longer care very much about the outcome, your performance can't help but suffer.

Unless you take steps to get back on track, one of two things will happen. You'll drift along until you either quit because you're being pressured to return to your previous level of performance, or you'll be fired.

While the value of physical exercise in reducing stress is important, this particular kind of stress responds better to counseling. If you need help, talk to a career counselor, a therapist, or even someone who has suffered from the same problem.

Before you pay anybody for help, find out if the person has dealt with burnout victims before. Ask for references. Nobody is a specialist in every problem. There are people in most parts of the country who have had some experience with the problem.

Find them. If you can't find anybody to help, here are some things you can do yourself.

1. Vary your routine at work as much as you can within the confines of our job. If nothing else, you can vary the time at which you do something or the way in which you do it or the order in which you tackle various tasks.

2. Reach out for contact with a group of people with whom you don't ordinarily associate. You need the new and different; you need other perspectives on work and life. You especially need people who are less intense than you are.

3. Start guarding your emotional energy. You can go through the motions of concern without spilling your guts or indulging in deep emotional involvement.

4. Enlist your family and friends in the cause. Don't spend time alone thinking about your problems. Talk to sympathetic listeners. Get feedback. Let these people show their concern.

5. Ask for reassignment in your job. If you're selling one kind of product or service, try to get transferred to selling another. Don't expect to get a promotion at this time. You're doing this to save your career, not advance it.

6. Reject the efforts of family and friends to use you as a sponge for problems until you've stabilized your own emotional situation. Once you're feeling better, you can get into other people's problems. In your present state, you can't be of much help anyway.

7. Talk about your feelings with someone who's not going through the same problems at the same time. If this doesn't help, assemble a group of burn-out victims and talk together for mutual comfort and support.

8. Don't kid yourself. You are not going to be burned out one day and full of ginger the next. It took time for you to get into this state and it'll take time to recover.

9. Examine your attitudes. Are you really indispensable to a particular group of clients? Will someone's whole life be ruined by your decision? If so, you're going to have to pace yourself in dealing with this kind of intensity. If you can't do that, you're not going to be able to work in your profession. A doctor said, as he resigned from his position in a hospital, "I'm going to Papua to lounge on the beach, to think, and to rest. I may never return to the practice of medicine." Happily, he exhausted the pleasures of both idleness and Papua in three months and returned to work, much refreshed. He now takes more frequent vacations and tries to slack off when he feels the return of his old burnout syndrome.

Don't tell yourself that if you didn't do it, it wouldn't get done. You are not indispensable. Remember, the choice is between functioning at a somewhat less intense level or not at all.

10. Don't suffer in silence. Discuss as much of what's happening with your boss as you think is politic. He or she has a stake in your mental health as well as your performance.

11. Take more, but shorter, vacations. Maybe you need six four-day vacations a year instead of a one-, two-, or three-week blowout.

12. Change jobs. There are higher pressure and lower pressure pockets even in the same job category. Investigate. Don't indulge in the "shoulds." Nobody can say that you "shouldn't" feel burned out. You do and that's a fact.

13. Change careers. There are all kinds of job and career possibilities that you haven't explored. If burnout is a recurring problem, you may need to rethink your career path. Pressure and high emotional involvement may not be your best act. Find out what is.

Don't be surprised if you have recurring but shorter bouts of burnout. That is the price of working with people, especially in any kind of traditional helping or client relationship. No one can tell you when you've had enough. Pacing, diversion, and flexibility can help postpone burnout, but nothing can prevent it entirely.

If you don't recognize the symptoms and deal

with them at once, you'll pay with your career, or, even worse, with a great deal of damage to your family and social relationhsips.

Fortunately no one gets hit by all three Killer Bs at once. Sometimes, however, they're progressive; you can't move up; you're bored; eventually you are burned out. You can also be burned out without ever having been blocked or bored. That's why you need to separate and treat only the problem you've got at this time.

Chapter 10
Obsolescence

Nobody sets out to become obsolete in a way that threatens his or her career, anymore than an actress or actor decides it would be fun to be a "has-been." Actors dread it, but the media continue to point out when an actor is through or on the way out. The media give the actors feedback so that they can prepare themselves.

Not so for the ordinary worker. There is no watchdog to point out when one specific worker has become obsolete. Yet our research indicates that most workers will become obsolete at some point in their professional lives, often without realizing what's happening. The only substantial signal may be a slowing down or stoppage of his or her professional advancement. That's not a sure sign, however, because in any recession, whether national or local, some fully productive workers fail to advance.

There may be no organizational signal of professional or organizational obsolescence. A person may be fired, phased out, refocused, or reassigned, even given early retirement if possible. No reason need be given. Some managers refuse to discuss obsolescence with a worker as a face-saving measure. It's a real career knockout because you may not find out that the organization, or your boss, has judged you obsolete until it's much too late for you to respond. In fact, you may be kept on the payroll out of a sense of paternalism or organizational inertia. Or you may be kept, not because you're productive, but because your boss is trying to keep as many jobs under his or her control as possible. Even though you lack anything approaching enough work to do, you will be kept. Complaining that you haven't enough to do and that you are losing your technical edge will only annoy your boss. Since the boss's goals in this situation are vastly different from yours, you may be in a position of enforced obsolescence. Your boss is making it very difficult for you to keep abreast.

This is more of a political than a skills problem. The person who faces obsolescence because his or her boss is playing a different game is not in the same spot as the individuals with whom we are concerned in this chapter.

OBSOLESCENCE: PROFESSIONAL AND PERSONAL

There are two kinds of unplanned obsolence: professional and personal. Professional obsolescense means that the individual can't produce what is expected on the job. Personal obsolescence means that the worker's style is no longer appropriate and this affects work-style and productivity. It may also put barriers between the worker and others in the work environment, especially younger managers, who are often acutely sensitive to style issues. These people equate outward signs with inner attitudes. They are generally right.

Organizational obsolescence, which means that the function is no longer useful or needed and that the job is or should be abolished, is not our real concern. People displaced when a company ceases to produce a product and gets rid of the department rarely have trouble finding other organizations making the same or similar things. It may be somewhat more of a problem for unskilled laborers in a small town. It may even be a hardship to move your family and change your lifestyle. It's still quite different however, from our main concern—an individual's self- or organizationally-judged obsolescence.

People who have trained for a single profession or sought to perfect certain skills, highly technical people, and people who have depended exclusively on

225

interpersonal or political skills to move ahead without adequate experience or technical education may find themselves beginning to show symptoms of job obsolescence. No profession or job category is free of people in the process of becoming obsolete, or even of those who are already in that state.

As one woman reported, her family doctor, in whom she had had, up to that point, the greatest faith, looked puzzled one day when she mentioned something about a new drug she'd read about in *Family Circle*. It takes nothing away from the magazine to state that this is not a source used by most doctors to keep themselves abreast of innovations in pharmacy. Still, her doctor had no idea what she was talking about and appeared to be unfamiliar with the drug. It was the first clue she'd had that the man was so busy with his patients that he'd let himself fall behind. He was becoming professionally obsolete in a field that requires constant updating. Lawyers, engineers, writers, and dentists face the same demands on their time, sometimes with similar results.

To a degree, aging relates to obsolescence, but it's rarely the main cause. To become obsolete means to refuse to keep up with what is going on in your field. This may be a tacit refusal or active resistance, but it is always a choice.

IDENTIFYING THE OBSOLETE

There was widespread agreement among the 347 managers we interviewed that an obsolete worker can be identified in some of the following ways.

1. The worker does not keep abreast of what's new in the field. He or she is not active in any trade and professional associations. Therefore, there is not the constant exposure to what's new, which is one of the purposes of membership. Even if the employer picks up the tab for membership and meetings, the employee doesn't attend or, if forced, does so grudgingly.

2. The worker has withdrawn from the competition to move ahead, win points, or just interact in the workplace. He or she spends all of his or her time just doing the assigned job at the minimal level required. There is no attempt to make the job more interesting or to enlarge it. The job is a chore, something to be gotten through. There is little job satisfaction or sense of accomplishment.

The worker does not actually refuse to produce. He or she will do the job, but the boss always gets the unmistakable impression that there's a holding back and that the work is done grudgingly.

Many workers, if called to task, aren't the least bit shy about telling their bosses that they are producing. "I'm fulfilling my job description. I'm not interested in moving up, so why kill myself?"

3. Training opportunities are refused as a waste of time and money. "I know all about that," the person says when a superior suggests a seminar or meeting. The person never asks to attend such session. Needless to say, there is no intention of spending personal money on training or further education.

"We've been after Sam to catch up on audit sampling techniques but he won't budge—says he doesn't need to. Every time we enroll him in a seminar he develops a 'conflict' at the last minute and puts one of his subordinates in his place. By now, six people in his department have been through the new material but not Sam. He just keeps resisting."

4. The person surrounds himself or herself with people whose first loyalty is to them, not to the job or organization. People in that department are rewarded for loyalty first, performance second.

A manager obsessed with loyalty can do more to reduce productivity than an industrial saboteur. Nothing has to be said. Employees know the score. They react to what they perceive as their own long-term interests.

5. There is an obsession with being plugged into every conceivable internal grapevine. There must be no slip-ups in finding out in advance what top management plans to do. People who assist in this process are rewarded and there is no question in subordinates' minds as to what is expected. Information gathering, not productivity, produces raises.

Subordinates are in a bind because, as top management catches on to the game, it collectively and individually may try to dry up some sources of information the manager needs or wants. The boss's boss may decide to surprise people.

6. Constant searches are conducted to find ways to reduce both the expected level of productivity and the amount of time spent producing. The person wants to spend as little time doing his or her work as possible. Others occasionally interpret this as boredom, but that's not really the problem.

The person who is obsolete isn't aware of any possibility of job expansion or enrichment, nor would such knowledge be welcome.

7. The obsolescent one will try to cast in concrete the procedures that cover the way work is to be done. All deviations from these procedures will be noted because style is always more important to him or her than to his or her peers. Rigid techniques and procedures mean that no ideas or methods can sneak in or be introduced to bother him or her. This resistance to the new will extend to every aspect of the job. All new employees in the department will get an inordinate amount of training not in what they are to do, but in how they are to do it.

If the obsolete person is not a manager, the strategy is to sell the current procedure to all new employees. This must be done before anyone gets a chance to change anything or to present a different view. Obsolete workers are anxious to be on welcoming committees and orientation programs so that they can sell tradition at every turn. If it were discovered that a new way might be better, someone might expect change. By talking tradition, the person casts himself or herself in a better light than if he or she simply resisted change outright.

8. There is an increasing withdrawal from socialization with coworkers and a consequent loss of power. Socializing is seen, not as necessary and business-related, but as a waste of time. There is even an effort to discourage others from "wasting" time on these activities. As a result, the worker is not keeping up with the grapevine and loses the chance to mold or remold the news to keep his or her career going.

9. Career planning and goal setting are dismissed as frills. Who needs career planning if he or she knows a dead end has been reached? Another waste of time, career planning is for beginners only.

Not every worker suffers from all of these symptoms at the same time. If you see yourself in any of these descriptions, you may be traveling the road toward job obsolescence. It's a judgment that you'll have to make about yourself. Until you see your own problem, any strategy planning is premature.

YOUR BOSS VS. YOU

Keep in mind, however, that your judgment may be different from the judgment your boss or others in the organization make about you and your effectiveness. If you suspect that you have been judged obsolete, it's time to confirm this informally through the grapevine. Try to find out what happened to others who had the same problem. This will give you some idea of how much time you have to plan your next move.

The more technical your work, the more research-dependent or research-oriented the product or service you produce, the more likely you are to face obsolescence. It may be very difficult or even impossible for you to keep abreast of every new development. Your organization may even expect some obsolescence.

Clayton Reeser writing in the January 1977 *Personal Journal* pointed out that thousands of well-paid technical people start becoming obsolete every year and "enter a 20 to 25 year period of ever increasing obsolescence every year in the United States." No matter how the organizations see them, these people could catch up or find less "high tech" areas in which to exercise their skills. The choices are not all on the side of the company. Depending on the bureaucracy to find solutions for your particular problem is rarely satisfactory. It is also unrealistic. All of those new college graduates who are up on the latest theory overrun the organization at least twice a year just dying to replace you, and at a lower salary as well.

WHAT'S YOUR CHOICE?

Choice is the key issue. Most of the literature on obsolete people focuses on what the organization thinks or wants and on the painful process of getting rid of these people or rehabilitating them. Like a long-neglected inner-city house, they need more than a quick, surface paint job. It would be more helpful and to the point to find out how people become obsolete and why they make that choice.

From your point of view, it's your career you need to be concerned about, not the organization's profits. If you've been judged obsolete, the organization is already thinking about its own interests. Based on our research, virtually every person who had problems of obsolescence or who had the symptoms we described knew they had made a personal choice to stop keeping up. There was no rhetoric about the company's failure to provide opportunities to advance, no denial that they had fallen behind.

Most seemed to understand clearly that the choice had been made once and reaffirmed every time an opportunity to catch up was turned down. The train didn't just stop once; it was on a very slow milk run. Even the people whose companies had declared their jobs or functions obsolete were not too surprised. They had known that the product or service was in trouble or that somehow the function they were supposed to manage was not profitable or viable. The only people who felt they had been wronged were those who were clearly victims of mergers, sudden reorganizations, or other business cataclysms.

Catch Up or Obsolescence?

Most of the people in our research chose obsolescence as the alternative to change because they hoped no one would notice. Unless and until people see that to become obsolete in a job, profession, or even just within an organization, means to make a choice between that and change, it's impossible for anyone to see himself or herself as anything but a victim. That's why being called obsolete or feeling obsolete is such a career knockout. If you don't think you did it to yourself, there's no real need to change or to confront the underlying problem. It's simply an event outside your control that occurred.

Why do people make such a choice when it's so clearly damaging to their careers? Many even have to be helped to see the choice they made. They have carefully shielded themselves from this knowledge as long as possible. As long as only the tip of the iceberg shows, or as long as people keep identifying obsolescence as age-related ("Poor Fred, he's really slowed down," or, "Sally's fifty-five now—over the hill"), the opportunities for self-delusion are endless. As long as obsolescence is "out there," you'll never have to confront it.

What Computer Software?

Roger would never have called himself obsolete even though his boss had judged him so. After all, there were no problems in the data processing department. All the programs ran smoothly, churning out endless pieces of information on cue. The problem appeared one day when it was announced that a systems consulting firm was being engaged to overhaul the department as part of a cost-cutting effort.

In a meeting with his boss and the consultants, it was instantly clear that Roger had never even heard of most of the techniques proposed to revamp the software. He didn't have to say a thing. It wasn't the fact that he couldn't use any of the techniques proposed, it was not having heard of them that was the career killer.

Resistance to chance is the attitude of choice for those who want to be obsolete. Like any other attitude, it's subject to change if you want it to change. Grabbing hold of the problem is difficult because there's no clear difference between personal and professional obsolescence. Both types of obsolescence look the same, but they stem from different causes. Until you find out which kind is your particular problem, it won't help to talk about changing your attitude.

The Closet Rebel

Are you a closet rebel? Is becoming obsolete your way of resisting change? Maybe you didn't think the department should be reorganized, a division sold or purchased, or the product or service changed. Your response was to stop putting effort into the job. You simply decided to reduce your level of job involvement and job performance. Managers cite this as the single most common response people have to change. It's the organizational version of passive resistance. Change resisters aren't necessarily afraid that they can't compete in a changed work environment; they may even think themselves well-equipped to do so. They have simply decided not to do so while wanting to remain with the organization. Knowing that many companies are reluctant to fire displaced workers because they fear the effect on the employees they want to keep, the obsolescent ones see their way clear to a free ride.

Younger employees see this reluctance as a free ride too. They'll take the ride until they decide what career changes they want to make. Older ones see themselves coasting until retirement. In a boom economy, such assumptions were probably reasonable. Benevolence is a corporate style. In the 1980s, these assumptions are very risky, especially among younger workers who have reduced their loyalty to organizations. What they don't realize, because it usually isn't in the employee handbook, is that organizations are reducing their levels of loyalty to workers. Loyalty is simply too expensive. It is gradually being taken out of the equation on both sides and its the individual who's likely to feel the effects first.

The Ostrich

You foresaw a major market or population change that was then some years in the future. You decided to ride it out to the bitter end before retooling. Consider how long it's been known that the number of school-age children is rapidly declining and you will see that teacher layoffs were predictable ten years ago. The teachers who waited to be laid off made a conscious choice; they chose to become obsolete. The only other assumption would be that teachers cannot read and that seems unthinkable.

The ones who chose to retool began doing so ten years ago. They knew that the numbers were against them, especially in the major metropolitan areas. No cries of foul play from them. They could and did read the endless stream of population projections published by the media; they acted on the information. Another group decided it would rather teach to the bitter end and then retool full-time. No cries from them either. But the great majority, who are trying to protect their jobs in the face of a vastly changed market, are those who refused to change. They created their own obsolescence problem.

"I've Got to Be Me"

There is also a whole subpopulation that says, "I don't care if values have changed. This is what I'm going to do." They don't quibble about labels. If there were never to be another paid concert in the United States, there would still be musicians and music students preparing for nonexistent careers. The same would be true of other artists. These people don't care if they seem obsolete and out of tune with market realities. They see no particular relationship between interests and making a living. Shifts in the economy mean little because they are tenaciously intent on doing what they like.

FORCED CAREER CHANGERS

Some of the obsolete are nascent career changers. They really don't want to do the job or even be in that field anymore. "I knew I had fallen behind," Eric said. "I wasn't even trying to keep up because all my effort had to be concentrated on the new business I was building. I was just hanging on to the job until my own business could carry me."

But for many people, changing careers is a problem requiring a whole raft of decisions. Obsolescence is a way of avoiding the real problem, of staying on the payroll, and of eventually changing by being forced to do so. These people see being laid off as a needed push.

Obsolescence may reflect your response to your own growing boredom with the organization, the specific work environment, or even the industry. You're no longer interested enough to keep up. It's too much trouble. You find the only thing that inspires you is the paycheck. You're satisfied to do as little as possible. You may be working for a company that is going through organizationally what you're going through individually; all the initiative has passed elsewhere.

This happens frequently to nonprofit groups that help solve the particular problem they were created to solve. None likes to simply dissolve—suicide is supposed to follow failure, not success. Having succeeded, they seem to settle in to fight a rearguard action to keep going until they can find another cause or until they run out of funds.

Your interests have changed. You no longer share the values and needs of your peers. The interests of the organization may have changed with a resultant shift in employee values. This change isn't really noticeable, but it accounts for some of your withdrawal from the group.

You may not appear to have changed in any way. Your outward appearance and mannerisms remain the same, but inside you're a different person. Some event in your life, or simply the process of living, has rearranged your inner landscape.

Your lifestyle may interfere with your keeping up. All of your attention and energy are focused elsewhere. The absorbing passion in your life is what you do from five to nine, not the reverse. This passion may be family, hobby, or simply passion. It is simply too much bother to keep up with your job and the changes in your field.

You may not have realized at what exact moment you ceased to take an active, growth-oriented interest in what you were doing. No one can pinpoint the exact time at which he or she decided not to compete. The organization and your boss probably couldn't do so either. However, as you think back, that date or aproximate date is the beginning of your career crisis. Trying to fix the date should also give you an idea of how far behind you are. If you have no idea, because you have been becoming more obsolete each year, assume the worst. You have a lot of catching up to do if that's what you decide you want to do.

Most people's recognition of just how far out of touch they are is precipitated by a question. Your boss mentions something with which you should be familiar, the industry's new hot/hot theory, and you draw a blank. You're often asked what you think about things you have never really heard of. The danger point is reached when people stop asking you because they can predict your answer; that's the point of no return. Once you have been passed over, only a great effort will help you catch up. You're no longer getting clues as to the areas in which you're weak.

CHANGE OR STAGNATE?

It must be clear by now that the minute you stop growing in your job, obsolescence sets in. Despite all you've heard about career plateaus, there is no plateau. A career plateau would mean being in the same job without moving up or out, for an extended period of time; plateaus are not supposed to include stagnating on the job. If they did, every worker working at a job more than two years might opt for early retirement on the payroll. Forget about plateaus. Once you stop creating your own excitement in a particular job, obsolescence sets in.

This idea is at odds with a favorite myth about work, the myth of sustained performance. According to the myth, the organization has no right to squawk as long as you do your job and nobody can actually hear your brain cells going numb. Don't be surprised if the organization rejects the employee's version of this myth.

What is the cost of choosing to be obsolete? If you have decided, consciously or not, that you're going to tread water and put no extra effort into your job, what are you risking? Most important is that you are sidelining yourself. Even if you don't want to go up, but do want to stay where you are, you'll have to keep up and continue working as if you were bucking for promotion. You can always turn down any unwanted offers. There is no such thing as maintenance-level job performance. Much of your problem may be that you simply aren't interested enough in the job to change the job, your style, or your attitudes. If that's the case, be aware that there is a limit to organizational tolerance. Your choice of maintenance is likely to be short-lived. The first real economic bump is going to bounce you out.

We interviewed fifty people who identified themselves as obsolete or who concurred with bosses who had made that identification. Overwhelmingly, they talked in terms of sticking it out or making do; that is maintenance. They made no effort to improve performance, to update their skills, or to raise their energy level.

The second problem in choosing obsolescence is that there is a real question of whether or not you could catch up, particularly if you've been sliding along for several years in a highly technical field. Can an engineer with ten years' experience in one area bring himself back to state of the art in that field? How much effort will it take? Can doctors and lawyers catch up if they've let themselves slide? Is it worth the massive effort it would take?

HIGH-COST CHOICES

The cost of choosing obsolescence in a bad economy is going to be very high. Even if there's no precedent, you will find out how your organization deals with obsolete workers when it deals with you. The organization may not have a firm policy, and it may become your boss's decision. You may be fired, permanently side-tracked, have your salary reduced, be reassigned to a lesser job at the same salary, or be forced to retire early. The boss will probably ignore the problem until forced by others to do something. A personal cost may be that he or she will judge you as being incompetent, not just out of sync. You may have to face a period of job insecurity. You may lose face with peers in a public demotion.

Are You Incompetent?

Few people adjust well to being thought incompetent or to being ignored, as if their opinions didn't matter. By swallowing all of the things you'd like to say in response to signals from superiors, peers, and subordinates, you're tacitly agreeing with and confirming those opinions. The only way you can fight back is to change. Thus you're caught between two distasteful alternatives. In the end, you'll either leave or be forced out as your self-esteem begins to match the esteem in which you're held by others. This is about the worst thing that can happen—in many ways more demoralizing than being fired. At least being fired is a clean, if final, solution.

MINISKIRTS AND PINK SHIRTS

Let's look at personal obsolescence for a minute since people with job obsolescence are frequently afflicted with personal obsolescence too. It can be an age-related kind of obsolescence, though it certainly doesn't have to be. Personal obsolescence means that you've adopted rigidity as your personal style. You are resisting change on a personal, as well as professional, level. For example, if you're female, you may still be wearing the teased hair and pointed toes of the late fifties and early sixties. If a man, you may be continuing to wear leisure suits long after they have been pronounced dead even in the most hinter of the hinterlands. You can tell this has happened when even the Salvation Army refuses to accept leisure suits for resale; anything the Salvation Army rejects is the pluperfect of obsolete. But you are determined to maintain your own personal style in whatever time warp you happen to have gotten caught.

There's nothing morally wrong with "bubble" hairdos, but the way you've chosen to package yourself on the job is seen as a reflection of your attitudes in general, including those that reflect in job performance. If you don't or won't change, even slowly and reluctantly, in response to changes in taste, your boss is likely to view your resistance as symptomatic of your attitudes toward work. This will be true even if your boss is personally obsolete. Rigidity is unattractive in everybody but auditors and cloistered religious orders.

Rigidity is fatal in the ordinary working world. It's a sign that every change that comes along will meet spirited resistance; you'll oppose everything on an ad hoc basis. This has nothing to do with personal or ethical standards. Length of hair, skirts, and lunch hours is not a moral issue; it's not something that even the cleverest manipulator can raise to an issue of principle.

Nobody will try to pull or push you closer to the center of group consensus. If you insist on hanging out on one end or the other of the bell curve, no one can stop you. Like the man who insists on keeping his shoulder-length hair long after it has ceased to make a social statement or the woman who won't give up her miniskirt, you are calling attention to yourself in the least favorable way. People are judging you by your nonverbal, as well as verbal, statements.

On the Soapbox

You can express your rigidity and brittleness in other ways. Witness the man of forty with many under-thirty subordinates who never fails to rail against the evils of marijuana even though he knows, or might assume, that many of the people who hear him are either users or have been in the past. It doesn't change their behavior in the least, but it does mark him as out of touch and judgmental.

What do you do if you are caught in some form of creeping obsolescence? You can't force others to make allowances unless you try nonstop, wall-to-wall charisma. If you really have that, you may want to turn to another chapter or skip all but the last chapter of this book. Your authentic choices are that you can change your attitudes or your style, play catch-up, or move on. You cannot change the response of those around you unless you change the material to which they can respond. Change is your real choice.

Matching Styles

If you decide to change your job or career, you may want to identify organizations that have a style similar to your own. You would not have been identified as obsolete unless you were out of sync with those around you. You would not be personally obsolete unless you were infringing on the tastes and styles of others. There are still organizations that collectively, or in isolated pockets, have a greater tolerance for personal style than does the one you're currently with. If you're with an organization that's technically representative of all that's current, you could move to one that is viable but not as progressive. If your personal style is too rigid for your present organization, locate one with more people like you. Even if you're willing to retool, you may find that moving to a less sophisticated environment will give you the time to do so. It may also give you some thinking time.

There is one step you must take if you have any hopes of catching up. You are going to have to become active in—attend meetings of and generally interact with people in—your trade or professional association. Make up your mind right now that trade and professional associations are the key to resisting stagnation and obsolescence. Unless you become and stay active in one, you're always teetering on the brink of professional disaster. This has been a well-kept secret because so many people have thought they could do without the associations. That is, they thought so until they tried it. There is no way to avoid this involvement. Staying away means you won't know where to begin your update. You could go to the library and read all the back issues of the professional journals you've been avoiding, but you'd still be behind because they're behind. It's inevitable that there will be a lag between the time something changes or an important breakthrough occurs and the time somebody writes about it coherently enough to get published in a trade or association journal. Don't kid yourself about this.

245

You must put your finger on the pulse of your profession or job interest and connect as firmly and quickly as you can.

If you're changing careers, you're even more in need of the associations. This time you need the ones in the field or profession you plan to join. They are your key to making the change, to being able to use the language of the new industry or job category you plan to join. The difference between an aspiring amateur and a member of a profession's "in group" is attitude and jargon. Learn the jargon and you'll have fewer problems penetrating the "in group" and convincing them that you're a peer.

What if you are up-to-date but are not perceived as being so by your boss? There has to be a reason for your boss's attitude. This is not the same thing as being seen as politically inept. If your boss thinks you're obsolete, you must find out why. Now is the time to start asking the kind of questions that will give you some clue as to the reason. Your first request should be for a detailed performance appraisal. If this is refused, your problem is political. In that case, update your résumé. Don't settle for vagueness; that's fatal to your career and can further damage your self-esteem. Get the facts, distorted as they may prove to be. You may not agree with the way your boss outlines a certain set of facts or perceptions, but you will have to take his or her interpretation into account. The decision as to how to deal with your obsolescence, whether it is real or only imagined by others, is entirely up to you. A bum rap means that you've been having political problems of which you weren't aware. If you really are obsolescent and have fallen down on the job, you've got to take corrective action immediately or plan to move on.

Chapter 11
Aging and Change

Ever since the passage of the Age Discrimination in Employment Act (ADEA) of 1967, amended in April of 1977, outlawing mandatory retirement before age seventy, many companies have been looking at workers over forty under a hostile microscope. These organizations are searching for workers whose performance, attitude, and measurable productivity have slipped because they want a legal reason to get workers short of the voluntary retirement age off the payroll. Waiting for a worker of forty-five to retire at age seventy seems like an eternity.

In the past, involuntary, or almost involuntary, early retirement took care of long-term workers whose performance had declined or ceased altogether. Good old Harry, who had been on the job for twenty-five years, began to slack off after age fifty. It was not too difficult to keep him until he reached fifty-five and then retire him. This policy was good for morale. Other older employees approved. They recognized that Harry had already decided to retire but that he was doing it on the company's premises with full salary and benefits.

From the workers' point of view, the organization showed its concern for its loyal people by tolerating Harry for a few years and then retiring him with full honors. Other employees looked forward to the same treatment in their declining years. Younger people were delighted because Harry's departure created an opening. If Harry didn't actually want to retire, it was just too bad for him. After all, organizational loyalty can only stretch so far. Good-bye, Harry.

The ADEA changed all that. Now Harry can sue for reinstatement and financial damages *unless* the company can show evidence of unsatisfactory performance. If his boss gave Harry satisfactory performance appraisals for twenty years, it might be difficult to prove Harry's sudden incompetence. This also rules out a boss's acting on the feeling of top management that someone has slowed down or on the consensus of others that someone should retire. Evidence may include comparisons with younger workers doing the same job. The organization will have to show that all workers doing one particular kind of job are judged by the same or similar performance standards. As long as Harry is healthy enough to do his work and performs, he will be hard to get rid of if he doesn't want to go.

FOCUS ON PERFORMANCE

Organizations have responded with a much closer examination of the forty-plus worker. They know that they will be stuck with all of the good old Harrys they accumulate over time until these people reach seventy. Companies that had been lax in performance appraisals on older workers are now conducting them with a vengeance.

"It's just like being a new employee all over again," reported a woman of fifty-three. "I feel as if I am on probation. I know my boss is looking for a reason to get rid of me and bring in someone younger. So far he hasn't had any reason—but he'll keep looking. It's a nightmare."

One company acknowledged that even though employees over fifty might still be productive, they had been dropped out of the promotion track except for very top management positions. "Except for the top seven officers in the company, the job you have at fifty is the one you will have when you retire," the personnel director said. This kind of policy will become increasingly difficult to defend in many large organizations, especially if people in lesser jobs want to move up. Needless to say, there's no room for late bloomers. It's no wonder Ray Kroc (McDonald's hamburgers) began his own business; at fifty-five he was organizationally over the hill.

The problems aging workers face aren't new. Until quite recently, most companies concentrated services to this group in the areas of pension planning, preretirement seminars including financial planning, and generally easing their transition out of the organization. To the extent that many workers resist retirement at sixty-five, strategies will have to change. Of course, there are some companies that have kept productive golden agers working through their seventies and into their eighties.

PRODUCE OR DEPART

From the organization's view, the problem is primarily one of getting rid of older workers who slow down or become totally unproductive. Companies have to comply with the law without letting productivity slide. This will become an ever more acute problem as the baby boom group ages. Sometimes there's a desire to dump productive middle-agers because places are needed to anchor bright new people to the organization. The younger ones may not be better workers, but they are almost always cheaper. All of those annual increases, merit reviews, and cost-of-living adjustments take a toll. Finances also help create pressure to force early retirement on marginal workers who are fifty-five or older.

Workers who resist being pushed out now have some legal redress unless their employers can prove a decline in performance. From the individual worker's point of view, however, the problem is not one of resisting retirement or even of seeking legal redress; it's the jungle of conflicting emotions people over forty face in making important career decisions. "Should I retire? What about inflation? Have I gotten as far as I'll ever get? Can I stand the pressure to perform and the feeling that I'm not wanted?"

THE OVER-FORTY MYTH

One of the reasons people in their late thirties often appear so frenetic is that The Myth is about to overtake their careers. The Myth says that if you are not very securely settled in a job by the time you are forty, it's all over. Your prospects evaporate and you enter the world of Dorian Gray. If you're fired, you'll never get another job. If you do get another job, it won't pay as well as the last one you had and you won't have the same title. It doesn't matter what kind of job the over-forty worker has; assembly-line workers and vice presidents have the same fears.

Many otherwise rational people behave as if they imagined that there were camps somewhere, maybe in Arizona and New Mexico, to which unemployed over-forty workers were sent. Why are these people sent away? The scenario doesn't cover that. It's probably so that none of the people who are over forty and unemployed will have to die of embarrassment, frustration, or despair in public. All camp inmates can commiserate with each other.

Witness the growth of over-forty employment support groups. Sometimes the groups include people so dispirited and depressed that they could be called nonsupport groups. That many people pooling their nightmares is bound to darken the atmosphere. Many people between forty and fifty will do literally anything to avoid being fired or laid off. The prospect of unemployment is a waking, unending nightmare because they believe in The Myth.

No matter how successful a person's career is at present, The Myth is always lurking in the background. "What would happen if I lost my job? Would I ever get another one?" The *Wall Street Journal* fuels this terror by occasionally running a Column One (front page) story about some man with years of experience, a great background, and all kinds of skills to offer, who, presumably because he is over fifty, has been unemployed for a year and a half or two years. The local newspapers also run such stories. There has even been a television movie about the problems an older man faced because of a long period of unemployment. None of his peers watched the program to see if there was a happy ending—if the man got another, comparable job. They knew, or thought they knew, that a happy ending wasn't even a possibility.

The Younger the Better

There is no denying that age discrimination exists. Many companies worship youth, but the government is watching. As one government official said,

"I look forward to the day when the X Company's sales manager will not have to worry about an occasional beard simply because no one on the sales staff will be old enough to shave!"

An advertising executive voiced his concern about the frantic youth orientation of his industry when he observed that "there may be a problem with a twenty-two-year-old's advertising campaign for a product aimed at a menopausal baby boom audience. I don't know that for sure, but I'm uneasy."

Not only are young people less expensive, they are supposed to be endowed with fresh ideas. They are said to be more productive. The young are alleged to be more flexible, easier to get along with, and easier to mold, not to mention better educated. This last is the most surprising contention of all because there are any number of studies to suggest that the "grade inflation" of the Vietnam War era has not ended in many colleges, especially in anemic programs desperate for students. The pressure for higher grading curves, put on by students, continues also. How else can Sue and Jack get into a good graduate business school? Their futures could be ruined! The assertion that the young are better educated doesn't hold water if you're talking in terms of how well versed in the basics such as grammar and written communication skills these people are compared to those who graduated a generation ago. Still, the illusion of better educated youth conditions employment realities.

Our concern, as always, is with strategies the

worker can use. Regardless of the legislation en-acted against age discrimination, the most effective remedies are those the individual worker enlists in his or her own behalf.

Aging can be a career knockout. This is true not just because discrimination keeps one individual from getting a job or promotion as quickly as that individual would like but because The Myth casts such a specter of fear over so many workers in that age group. In a youth-obsessed society, one that worships the new, the fresh, arriving at forty is a personal knockout, not just a career problem. This has been documented endlessly by both popular and academic sociologists.

Facing aging and its impact on careers, the indi-vidual faces a second whammy. Society tells him or her that he or she is personally over the hill. No wonder people begin to worry obsessively about their careers.

LOSS OF COMPETITIVENESS

The worker's productivity may not change at all. He or she may be consistently more productive than younger people doing the same job. Skills may still be state of the art. Experience is an asset. What does change and what is obvious to many employers is attitude. There is a loss of competitiveness and a drop in professional confidence. It takes only one mention of some new and unfamiliar theory, espe-cially if introduced by a twenty-five-year-old, to trigger a process of snowballing self-doubt. That's the real career killer. If this were not untrue, if most people over forty really did hit a slide in productivity, businesses would be screaming for mandatory retirement at age forty-five.

In interviewing some 250 over-forty workers, the problem of self-doubt beaame all too clear. "I keep wondering if I'm still competitive, if I still have what I had at thirty." Or, "I wake up sometimes in the middle of the night and ask myself what I'd do if I lost my job because I may not perform as well as I think I do. A new employer might pick that up."

The middle manager whose skill is managing people rather than technical expertise is especially prone to this worry. "What if a prospective employer doesn't think experience is worth anything?" These people have an inordinate fear of reorganizations, mergers, cutbacks, anything that might loosen the hold they have on one particular job.

In the past, a great many workers worried that they'd be fired just before their pension rights were vested. That was the nightmare of the 1950s. Some companies, in an attempt to hold down pension costs, did fire workers right before they reached fifty-five. They did this regardless of the individual's length of service or the quality of his or her work. It meant that the individual would get either no pension or a much smaller one than he or she had been expecting.

In fairness to employers, the absolute number of such cases was far smaller than the over-forty crowd supposed. However, just one documented case was horrifying enough to permanently demoralize everyone who heard the story. Certainly everyone of a certain age at the company where the incident took place shuddered.

With pension reform legislation, which forced most companies to either vest the employee fully after a certain period of time, usually ten years, or get rid of its pension plan altogether, such fears have become a lesser problem. Now the main worry is The Myth—loss of the job.

The over-forty set has a very effective network. Each rumor of someone who couldn't get another job after reaching fifty leaves a few peers trembling. Like a stone tossed into still water, the eddies fade very slowly. Job security becomes an obsession; it completely obscures every other issue, including work satisfaction, personal and professional growth, and advancement. As a result, much of the energy that should be devoted to those issues goes into worrying full-time about termination.

It becomes not, as some employers claim, a process of people in their forties and fifties trying to retire on the job, but a nonstop scramble to anchor themselves to the organization with unbreakable ties. It's amazing how far people will go. A single man of fifty with a paid-up whole-life insurance policy offered the university where he worked a deal. He'd name the school as beneficiary on the policy if he retired from the university at age sixty-five. Universities, always loath to turn down donors, loved the arrangement. It worked.

That kind of bribery won't work with most organizations. There are enough documented examples to suggest that, if an organization has an informal policy of age discrimination, nothing short of class action suits will make a difference. These are expensive, time consuming, emotionally bruising, and not very helpful to one individual tangled in the process. A better strategy is individual action. This allows each person to make the career decisions that will secure his or her career. Always keep in mind that there is no absolute job security for anyone, anytime, anywhere.

The time to begin planning to meet the problems of the forties and fifties is in the thirties. So many people at thirty-five push off the traumas they see down the road, perhaps hoping that none will catch up with them. Maybe they think that enjoying today is more important, especially if they see The Myth over the next hill. If some career planning is done in the thirties and some options secured, the forties and fifties could be significantly less worrisome, even satisfying.

WHAT OPPORTUNITIES?

If you are approaching forty, or have passed into the land of The Myth, now is the time to begin looking at your career opportunities. If you want to work until you are seventy or older, the decisions you make now are critical. Nothing could be more foolish than waiting until you reach a crisis—your job in danger for instance—and then blindly scrambling. You must do your planning before you're in danger. Otherwise you could spend ten or twenty years obsessed with what you see as the shakiness of your hold on your job, victimized by your fears and lack of alternatives.

Before you can list options, you must examine your present job. Are you as competent, as current in your field, as the younger ones coming in now? If not, why not? Are you coasting on the theory that you will be kept by the company simply because of your years of service? This is the most dangerous assumption you could make. In the economic uncertainty of the 1980s, which even the federal government predicts will be a period of "negative growth," loyalty will mean absolutely nothing. Productivity and competitive advantage will count for everything.

The younger worker has already realized that loyalty and job longevity mean nothing to employers and has acted accordingly. These values seldom mean anything to young workers who are using a variety of tactics to make themselves as mobile and independent of any individual employer as possible. The attitude of new MBAs is that they are "guns for hire," the Paladins of the corporate world. Non-profit organizations, caught in a crippling inflation squeeze, are adopting corporate attitudes toward getting rid of the unproductive. They can no longer afford to provide absolute job security for employees. The less you count on an advantage based on your organizational loyalty, the better. In an economic crisis, loyalty may buy you an extra week or two on the payroll, that's all. You'll still end up on the street.

Second, does your organization have a tacit policy of age discrimination? How many people older than you are in the organization? If you are among the oldest, regardless of salary level, be aware that top management has an agenda that includes either not hiring or getting rid of older workers. What is the average age of people hired into the organization at all levels? Does anyone over forty slip through or is a "more qualified" candidate turned up?

Service and knowledge workers are not engaged in activities requiring brute strength. Older workers are no less able to think and reason than younger ones. Your management has a deliberate policy of keeping the organization young if few over-forties are hired or promoted. Some companies call this keeping the company "green." It then becomes a question of how young they propose to keep it. Personnel departments are an absolute mirror image of the tastes and prejudices of top management. They recruit the people who please top management. If the word is out that the organization likes molding the young rather than taking in experienced workers, your job may be in danger. Remember, if affirmative action and the EEOC have taught top management anything, it has been not to talk about the hidden values within the organization. Management has to be more subtle, even if they are doing something illegal. Also remember that someone who is determined to get rid of you, whatever the reason, will find a way to do so.

If you look around and find that you stand out or that you have few age peers, it may be time to develop some new strategies. If you were forced to move suddenly, where would you go? Have you thought in terms of a different company, a second career, starting your own business, going back to school? If any of these appealed to you in the past, make more specific inquiries. Why wait until you're called into the boss's office for the last conference?

SECOND CAREER?

Male or female, if you think your position may become shaky in a few years, begin planning your next move now. Get a line on your organization's competitors. Which of them is doing best financially? Are there any smaller companies that would welcome your sophistication and expertise?

If you are primarily a manager and not a technical specialist who's moved into management, you may want to consider smaller companies, possible even start-up companies, very carefully. Remember that start-up companies frequently need sophisticated management. They have an idea, a process, something with market value, but they frequently lack managerial backup. These companies are a part of the submerged, even disguised, job market. You can't ferret them out in one afternoon at the library.

Begin reading all of the trade journals in your particular industry or in the industry you think you would like to join. It may take you several months to become familiar enough with the characteristics of these companies to choose the ones you'd like to approach. It's well worth the effort. You may find an organization not only eager to hire you but willing to toss a piece of the action into the pot. What better hedge could there be against inflation and old age?

If you're planning on a second career, begin now to develop the expertise or additional skills you'll need. If you're thinking of your own business, contact the Small Business Administration. Attend some of their seminars and find out what's involved in opening your own place. If you wait until you're under the pressure of imminent dismissal, you'll be unable to make quality decisions. This is your time for planning and experimentation. It's a whole new, potentially exciting and rewarding ball game. You may surprise yourself when you learn that you're not dead yet. Press on.

Whatever you do, don't sit like a lump in your present job and wait for the axe to fall. It's amazing how many people, instead of looking outward to see what else may be available, look inward to see what they can do to shore up the present job. Accept the fact that this can't always be done. If you concentrate on trying to anchor yourself to a hopeless situation, you're wasting effort and precious resources. You're responsible for frustrating yourself Don't do it.

THE UNTAPPED RESOURCE

If you are a man with a wife who does not work outside the home, you have a priceless untapped resource. If you wife has not worked for a paycheck in years, perhaps never, it's time to talk about that. Sit down and have a frank discussion about her work and your joint future. If your wife got some training and/or job counseling now, she could get a job. The money she earned would provide a backup in case anything happened to your job.

If you are still enamored of the "me Tarzan, you Jane" ideal, this may seem like an appalling idea. But, what other kind of "insurance," even peace of mind, can you buy? Any company will sell you a life or disability policy, but who will sell you a policy against long-term unemployment or job obsolescence?

A working wife is insurance against the anxiety and economic threats of The Myth. The growing number of two-income families signals a recognition of a change in probabilities more than of a change in values. A working wife provides a sense of security that does two things for you: 1) it buys you some thinking and planning time so that you can assess your career direction and prospects and 2) it reduces your sense of panic and insecurity so that your employer has less reason to bully you.

And employers do bully older workers. Not openly, of course; that would involve confrontation and acknowledgement. Many bosses feel no qualms in making the lives of the post-fifty crowd unpleasant, even if they are over fifty themselves. As one top executive said, "Where's he going to go? He's lucky to have a job with us. Who'd hire him at his age?" The boss reasons: poor Steve is tied to us economically, thus we can give him a smaller raise and he'll stay. This type of reasoning is an upfront part of the thinking of top management in many nonprofit organizations. Part of the reason a younger worker doing the same job may get a larger raise than you is the greater mobility that worker has. If the youngster isn't progressing at the rate he or she would like, he or she may leave. He or she is certainly able to do so, and management certainly knows it.

Once a man has a working wife, he's less likely to submit to any subtle blackmail or humiliation. He knows where the next mortgage payment is coming from and how he'll keep the kids in college. This allows him to negotiate from a position of greater strength. He's not likely to start a shouting match or to tell off the boss, but the boss will know about his strengthened position. That particular man is no longer completely subject to organizational whim in the same way he was.

Who knows how far a new working wife may go? She may take the bit in her teeth and decide to give her family genuine financial security single-handedly. Wives benefit personally from working as well. They stop pushing their husbands and begin pushing themselves. This reduces some of the tension and concern husbands feel during what is a difficult time anyway. Would you rather sit in the recreation room eyeball-to-eyeball waiting for the phone to ring with a job offer to have an assured income? Think how unlikely it is that both of you would be out of work at exactly the same time. Many women think of returning to work as their children grow up.

Many more might be encouraged to take this step if they understood what it could do for individual self-confidence and for family stability. It's the only form of independence and security the average couple can hope to have.

Women seem to face fewer age discrimination problems overall because affirmative action, though not concerned with age, focuses attention on women as a protected group. There are, of course, large pockets of age discrimination, particularly in the glamour industries. There aren't many older women in modeling, newscasting, reporting, fashion, etc. Still women over fifty seem not to have as many problems getting jobs. This includes the returning-to-work crowd. These women are often concentrated at entry level positions—second-time beginners.

As more women move higher up the economic

ladder, they can expect to meet the same age-related problems as men face. Again, the strategies men should use will also help women: 1) a working spouse, 2) early investigation of alternatives, and 3) action instead of reaction.

What of the single person over forty? How can one person alone shore up his or her financial position and buy some independence from The Myth? The best thing a single person can do is to begin financial planning at an early age, to develop second career options, to look at alternatives to the present job, and to maintain an extensive professional and personal network. There will be many more single adults over forty joining forces to buy property, provide mutual support, and develop different kinds of communal living arrangements independent of sexual relationships in the 1980s. This will be as much a result of economic necessity as of choice. As the cost of living skyrockets, housing costs will literally drive unrelated singles together. There are career advantages to be reaped from this.

Help is on the way. The baby boom crowd is going to be thinking about retirement at the turn of the century. Social security is not likely to provide much for such a huge group trying to collect at one time. These people, raised in the civil rights and women's movements, will be demanding and getting much more government assistance in breaking down age discrimination and retirement norms. Until then, each middle-ager will be pretty much on his or her own against the system. If enough people band together in class action suits, things may change more quickly.

In the interest of self-preservation, there can be nothing more important than choosing a job you'll enjoy doing well into your seventies. You may end up working that long. You should, if you're to be successful, indeed you must, enjoy what you do. Make your goal independence from any one organization—not a more adhesive hold on it.

Conclusion

Having seen all of the land mines, career knock-outs, and general pain and suffering waiting for the unwary, you as a worker trying to move up, move out, or just hold on will have your hands full. You could hardly be blamed if you decide that a career in a cloistered religious order has been vastly under-rated. Perhaps the people who are dropping out of the system know more than they are credited with. Take heart! Not all of these problems are going to face you, at least not all at the same time. It's unlikely that even two will happen at the same time.

Still, you do need to be aware of what can happen so that you can be alert to signs that any of these problems is about to befall you. The price of a successful, satisfying career is eternal watchfulness. It has always been that way and it always will be that way. We predict this with great confidence even though the Career Strategies crystal ball has been recalled for a major parts replacement. (It got cloudy at inopportune times.)

You do have certain assets that make it possible for you to look to your own future with a cautious optimism. If you have some knowledge of what has happened to other workers—and therefore could happen to you—you're in better shape than you were during the Dark Ages (say all of the time up to the present). Many of these problems have seldom been talked about. The conspiracy of silence that surrounded things such as a lack of working class or reverse discrimination, for instance, helped nobody. It was especially unhelpful for those who were faced with the problem. There is no point in pretending that bosses make, or ever have made, decisions about people in totally rational ways. If some of the irrational criteria they used were known, espeically the ones your boss applied to you, then you would have choices to make. You might decide to correct your real or imagined weaknesses or you could decide it's not worth it to you and move on. That is a perfectly valid choice. Having a choice is the most anyone can hope for in a very uncertain world.

You don't have to go along with people who make decisions on a whimsical or non-work-oriented basis.

You may decide to dedicate your working life to changing the system from within. Since you're probably going to work past the conventional retirement age of sixty or sixty-five, you should be able to accomplish a lot. It's great to want to change the system. But before you try to change it, it might be helpful to know what the system is and how it works. If you don't examine whatever system you are a part of, you may change the good without touching the bad. Career planning should help you make your examination; it should provide not only tools for change but also a road map of the present terrain.

The social revolution isn't over. Sexual and racial discrimination haven't been defeated by any means. Genuine equality of opportunity is still a long way off. However, things are changing for most victims of discrimination. Don't get discouraged. Unless you get involved and work for change within the system, the efforts of all the pioneers who paid so dearly for very small gains will be lost. These pioneers paid so much for even the modest opportunities you enjoy; most did so cheerfully. Don't relax your own efforts now. The economic problems of the 1980s could provide a perfect opportunity to reverse the trend in broadening opportunities for women and minorities.

And that's the real message of this book. There is no way to relax and move forward at the same time. You have nothing to look forward to if what you want to do is relax. Even the people who are busily exploring alternative lifestyles have discovered that they must alternate periods of coasting with periods of intense activity.

You are face-to-face with a genuine economic crisis in the 1980s. Unless you can find some more dinosaurs, suitably processed into oil, or persuade OPEC to lower oil prices, the energy crisis is going to condition all of your thinking and planning about your career. The lack of energy will profoundly affect your working life from now until the year 2000. You are going to learn to do without a great many things the generation of people before you thought they could not live without. This includes the right to waste scarce fuel and vacations in campers or boats that get seven gallons to the mile. You will survive this deprivation and make your own satisfying substitutes.

Part of the message of the 1980s is that what constitutes work satisfaction is going to move closer to the model of an earlier generation. More people are going to see that they must generate their own work satisfaction rather than depend on others to point out what's been done well. The emphasis is going to be on greater productivity, however that is measured, at lower cost. You are going to be more productive for less money. There is simply no other way to keep inflation at a manageable, if not comfortable, level. Your satisfaction with work may come from doing this, not to mention your job security and advancement. The number of nonproductive or marginally productive people any organization, especially a nonprofit organization, can afford to carry is going to decline dramatically.

The themes of the 1980s are going to be competency, productivity, and waste reduction. If you love a challenge, this is the decade for you. You'll have all that you can handle. Good luck and watch out for land mines!

BEST OF BUSINESS
FROM WARNER BOOKS

OFFICE POLITICS: Seizing Power, Wielding Clout
by Marilyn Moats Kennedy   (K93-718, $2.95)
Ms. Kennedy leads a crash course in the mastery of office politics: how to get to the top and how to stay there, how to recruit friends "upstairs" and how to use them. She advocates office politics, not as dirty backstabbing, but the way to get things done.

GETTING ORGANIZED
by Stephanie Winston   (J97-806, $5.95)
Guidelines to organization covering everything from financial to meal planning, maximization of storage space, living space and reduction of time required to complete everyday tasks.

GETTING ORGANIZED: Time and Paperwork
by Stephanie Winston   (J97-564, $2.50)
Extremely practical guidelines for simplifying and arranging one's time and demands made upon it. Ms. Winston provides checklists and charts to help teach anyone to use time to its maximum advantage and keep paperwork to a minimum.

WORKING SMART: How to Accomplish More in Half the Time
by Michael LeBoeuf   (K33-147, $2.95)
Mr. LeBoeuf applies his knowledge as a professor of Management, Organizational Behavior and Communication to helping people understand how to: increase effective use of time and energy, set goals and priorities, and eliminate anxiety and anger by being able to cope with everyday activities.

To order, use the coupon below. If you prefer to use your own stationery, please include complete title as well as book number and price. Allow 4 weeks for delivery.